Holistic TypeScript

Patrick Desjardins

Author: Patrick Desjardins

Self-Publishing

Email: mrdesjardins@gmail.com

Website: http://patrickdesjardins.com

Source code available: https://github.com/MrDesjardins/holistictypescript

Printed in the United States of America

Legal Deposit Statement:

Legal Deposit - Bibliothèque et Archives national du Québec, 2018

Legal Deposit - Bibliothèque et Archives national du Canada, 2018

ISBN-10: 2981311069
ISBN-13: 978-2981311061

DEDICATION

I dedicate this book to my wife, Mélodie Savaria, who has been patient during the time I took to write this book hereafter all other projects I am incubating. I also dedicate this work to my parents, who opened the path to all my realizations, present and future. Finally, I dedicate this book to my daughter Alicia, who I hope will never give up and always stretch beyond her dreams.

TABLE OF CONTENTS

ACKNOWLEDGMENTS

I wish to thank, first and foremost, everybody who has been patient with me during this process. I owe my deepest gratitude to those who challenged me at work, during conferences, and by their comments on my website. You have helped me to improve every day.

CHAPTER 1: HIGH-LEVEL VIEW

This chapter introduces the reasons for using TypeScript and the philosophy behind the superset. A quick comparison with the leading contender of TypeScript is presented to give a perspective on how TypeScript may or may not fit your requirement to use a static type checker. An excerpt of TypeScript's philosophy and principles is shared to position the tool against another popular static analyzer. The goal of this chapter is to provide accurate information about how you can use TypeScript in your projects. Also, it is but proper to share any information with a colleague who might not fully understand how a type checker may improve the velocity of a team and how quickly integration is possible into an existing JavaScript project.

1.1 WHAT IS TYPESCRIPT

TypeScript is a language on top of JavaScript. Everything possible in JavaScript is available in TypeScript – it is a superset of JavaScript. It provides two strong advantages. The first one is that it transpiles TypeScript into JavaScript which means that advanced ECMAScript features not available to all web browsers can be used by providing a polyfill. It acts as a combination of other static checkers combined with Babel. The second one is to enforce static typing that can catch potential issues earlier in the life-cycle of development. It reduces the need for some unit tests and can analyze the code to find runtime error at design time.

TypeScript has been made public since 1 October 2012, but its inception started at Redmond two years before as an internal product (2010) at Microsoft. The project is open source, hosted on Github.com under an Apache2 license.

TypeScript's popularity increases year after year. It has 317 branches, 228 contributors, 48 releases, 188 pull requests monthly created with over 3 600 forks and 25 000 stars. The consistent cadence of releasing a new version every two months and the great ecosystem of people contributing make it a stellar open source project that evolves rapidly to sustain developers' needs, as well as follow the rapid pace of web technologies.

TypeScript is far from being used only by its creator, Microsoft. While it's true that many Microsoft products use TypeScript, like Microsoft Teams, Visual Studio Team Services (VSTS), the online version of Office, Visual Studio Code (VSCode), to say the least, other technology giants have been borrowing the advantage of static typing. Google has been using it since Angular 2, Slack has migrated their JavasScript code base to TypeScript as well, and other companies like Ubisoft, Asana, Ericsson, Upwork, Bloomberg, and Lyft are also following. The reason I mention these systems that use TypeScript is to highlight the investment of thousands of developers and the millions of lines in these technologies. Most of them come from different backgrounds. Aside from the tremendous amount of work and knowledge poured across the industry, it illustrates that many people before you had to decide whether to go with TypeScript or not—and chose to do so. While most of the examples provided are big projects, they all do have one thing in common, i.e. some people must write and maintain the code. Static typing shines in these areas, from small to big projects.

Here is a quick note about who is leading TypeScript. Anders Hejlsberg manages TypeScript. He is the creator of Turbo Pascal, Delphi, C# and now TypeScript. Hejlsberg graduated in the '80s, has received many awards in his career, and is the person who made the most commits on GitHub on that project. Having such a prolific engineer at the head of TypeScript boosts the maturity of the language.

The TypeScript community is beyond the repository where it resides. StackOverflow's members are strong, with more than 35 000 questions. There are plenty of examples with TypeScript code with many different frameworks. It's not difficult to find Angular or React examples written in TypeScript or popular projects like the famous TodoMVC.

TypeScript is all about having a strongly typed language at design time, but the code produced doesn't contain any type. The type gets erased because Typescript removes types, interfaces, aliases at transpilation and end up with a common JavaScript file. The removal may sound logical but the lack of type at runtime results in a design that must not rely on the type dynamically at runtime. We will see examples of this when working on type comparisons to figure out the interface used. Keep in mind that interface and type are not available at runtime, hence how can this check be performed when the code executed is a challenge?

1.2 TYPESCRIPT PHILOSOPHY

TypeScript has a well-documented design goal which inspires developers who use TypeScript to follow the same philosophy. The main point is to identity the construct that will produce a runtime error.

Secondly, TypeScript's goal is to provide a structuring mechanism that can scale to a large code base. JavaScript on its own tend to become harder to maintain with a large number of different developers and a substantive amount of code. This second goal embraces the first one which allows modification and being notified of a potential issue as fast as possible. Types self-document the code and conscribe potential values to specific variables.

The third goal is not to impose overhead on the produced JavaScript. This goal goes hand in hand with the fourth goal, which to produce clean and recognizable JavaScript. TypeScript's final output is JavaScript code, and depending on the version you specified you want the output to be, will produce the most readable, efficient and clean code. The result would be humanly usable, which is not only a great way to experiment with TypeScript and be able to decide to stop and then to continue with JavaScript but is also a great way to debug.

The fifth goal is toward having a language that can grow well in the future by making it composable and easy to get around. Sixth, in the spirit of being future-compatible, TypeScript aims to be aligned with ECMAScript, not only with the current version but also with the future versions.

TypeScript doesn't try to supersede JavaScript, but being a good citizen, it never overrides existing behavior. Preserving runtime behavior makes TypeScript compatible with all existing JavaScript code, but is also a big leverage for an experimenting JavaScript developer who can start using TypeScript with the same known libraries and functions that they know. The eighth goal is to avoid adding expression-level syntax, which again preserves a syntax close to JavaScript without making it a completely new language.

TypeScript brings types, which means it needs to have a structured system (for example, interfaces, types, classes). However, the goal is to have this layer removed at runtime, again, ensuring an output completely compatible with ECMAScript.

While Microsoft worked hard to not be a walled garden behind a specific operating system, or browser, or any other constraint like IDE, TypeScript works on both Mac and Windows, and the output works in all browsers since it always follows the ECMAScript standard. It is also compatible with many development tools and doesn't favor anyone more than the other. TypeScript offers a tool that allows external IDE to communicate with it, which allows great extensibility for a third party.

Finally, TypeScript draws from the strength of Microsoft products which is to be backward-compatible. Caring about the past is a huge win and a paramount gain for a long-term project. What you are coding today will work in the future, and it is part of the core concept of TypeScript. However, backward compatibility has been true since version 1, and the TypeScript team works with the principle of not causing any substantial breaking change.

It's important to understand that TypeScript is not trying to create a perfect language on top of a flawed language that is JavaScript. It uses existing JavaScript behaviors and works with them. TypeScript is always swaying between being correct and being productive. The balance is important to keep developers' velocity high. TypeScript is not trying to be innovative and bring a new way of thinking how to develop but it leverages common patterns well known by many languages while keeping the flexibility of JavaScript.

1.3 REASONS TO USE TYPESCRIPT

TypeScript provides many advantages for client-side developers. In this section, we will see many reasons to use TypeScript.

TypeScript is not a completely new language. It is easier to pick up than some other alternatives since you can jump with a JavaScript background and learn how to use the enhancement that TypeScript offers.

TypeScript is fast. Even if it has a compilation phase called "transpile," it scales well with large code bases. You do not need to transpile every TypeScript file you have but you can transpile a subset, like a file that has changed, or a directory. Being fast is crucial to have a good flow while developing. JavaScript has the advantage of being a runtime language and having a middle ground which is not a burden; it reduces the friction for people with a habit of having fast results in their browser. Following that line of thought, automatic build on files change by a third party is available. The combination of TypeScript and other tools transform the experience into a quasi-seamless flow.

Transpiling allows you to generate ECMAScript, and TypeScript lets you specify which version is desired. The degree of detail means that you can generate JavaScript compatible with a very old browser or a new one, or with a feature that is planned to be available but not yet there. The output is a different JavaScript, depending on which target. This feature allows you to use modern TypeScript syntax; for example, "async" not being fully supported by all browsers today and targeting a version of ECMAScript that doesn't support it. TypeScript will remain the same since it borrows the ECMAScript standard syntax and the produced JavaScript will be different depending on the target. An old target version will provide polyfill—less performant but will still produce the same behavior for the user. Targeting a newer version leverages the native browser support of features and will be performant and will also produce a clean JavaScript. In the example of "async," it would use a Promise approach with an older version of ECMAScript that doesn't support it natively but would use the "async" syntax directly with the newest version.

TypeScript lets you use the libraries and framework you already know as a client-side developer. You can use JQuery, MomentJS, BootStrapJS, React, etc. There is no constraint. The interoperability is a huge win because you can transpose existing expertise without having to learn equivalences. Aside from lowering the barrier to entry, it makes TypeScript have the same ecosystem that JavaScript owns.

Furthermore, TypeScript uses the popular tool named NPM. NPM gives access to millions of libraries available and has been tested for many years, and they are accessible with a known and appreciated mechanism. Avoiding a custom tool to access libraries simplifies the jump to TypeScript by not having to learn a new language and a new tool. The same known NPM commands work with TypeScript to access definition files as well.

TypeScript brings static typing. To not be strict remains an available option. It's worth a wise choice at a moment when a hybrid model may be the only viable option. It is recommended when starting a new project to enable the strict mode which will enforce type. Nevertheless, having TypeScript letting you progressively add type is a nice touch for people who are just starting, to be able to bring TypeScript into an existing JavaScript project. The hybrid option can introduce static type slowly without having to halt existing development because of a huge migration. You can go at your pace. In fact, TypeScript can run against existing JavaScript code and even provide inference and a minimum set of validation in the boundary of what is realizable.

TypeScript is easier to refactor. The reason is related to static typing. If you rename a member, this one can be found everywhere it is used and hence rename every place. Changing a type will highlight incompatibility straight in the IDE you use or during compilation. This is true with many features like changing if a member is optional or not, or adding, removing or modifying parameters of a function. Navigation inside TypeScript code is a breeze since you can navigate to references of functions or members since IDE can link usage of specific types and their content.

In the same vein, TypeScript is easier to maintain, because reading the code is more obvious than JavaScript. For example, an object that initializes with an option would not explicitly define all the potential options in JavaScript. Normally, if you are new to the piece of code using a parameter that is an object, you need to look up inside the function and follow as much as you can, which can be deep, what is used inside the object. You could also look at the unit tests, or the documentation if they are available. In all cases, this is time-consuming. With TypeScript, you can look at the type, click on it and see the definition. It's quick, self-documented, and provides insight without digging.

TypeScript has a mechanism to define existing JavaScript library to have good support. It's called "definition file" which we will see in this book. The definition file is optional, but when provided to JavaScript library code, it brings Intellisense as well as type to untyped code. This increases the productivity of developers by reducing potential typos and bringing documentation at their fingertips, which reduces losing focus by switching to external documentation.

TypeScript has an excellent Intellisense. As mentioned, existing JavaScript libraries can get TypeScript typing and allow them to be with code-completion capability. Meanwhile, TypeScript by default is fully Intellisense-supported, which means that every type defined can be used with an experience that provides type members, function arguments, types and return, etc.

TypeScript reduces the number of unit tests. Checking for types (structures) or expected members on the object, or a type that passed by parameter for undefined and null value are all cases that TypeScript checks on compilation with static types. Less code means less code to maintain. The unit tests only focus on meaningful things like logic or actual algorithms.

JavaScript has many quirks, and TypeScript mitigates potential pitfalls that could only be found at runtime by exposing them at development time. TypeScript lets you fine-tune the rigidity of how it harnesses quirks for you. For example, the arithmetic with JavaScript is pretty loose; also, specific values can be interpreted during value comparison.

Finally, TypeScript is a low risk to take since it produces a human-readable JavaScript which is like an exit door wide open to start and stop in the future. It's a low risk since it is open source, which means that in the event that Microsoft stops maintaining the language, anyone could jump on it. That being said, Microsoft, Google, and other big corporations have invested millions in TypeScript, which should also be a good indicator for a smaller company that it is not a small project maintained by some part-time developers. Finally, the risk is low because the learning curve is gentle for a JavaScript developer.

1.4 COMPARED TO FLOW

Microsoft TypeScript has few contenders. Facebook Flow is one that is getting tractions recently, and since it is very similar to TypeScript, a few points of comparison can be interesting when you are looking to introduce a static typing tool for a project.

Flow was first made public on 18 November 2014, and TypeScript on 1 October 2012. But TypeScript has been in use two years before that as an internal product (2010). This information doesn't give us much else as to which one went through more active days of finding bugs or which might have had leverage on the pros and cons of the former. The difference in years between the two is relatively small, which makes both of them still young.

Flow started at Facebook; TypeScript at Microsoft. The motivation of Facebook was to create a system that was "sound", whereas TypeScript was not as sound with respect to how JavaScript behaved. Here is a quote from Microsoft TypeScript documentation: "In practice, this sort of error is rare, and allowing this enables many common JavaScript patterns." Microsoft's goals and non-goals are well defined. We can read: "Non-goal: apply a sound or provably correct type system. Instead, strike a balance between correctness and productivity." I'll provide more example of what it means later in this book. For this overview, let's just conclude that TypeScript is closer to JavaScript in some behaviors, while Flow is closer for this matter to Java or C# by being more strict. The idea of which one is better is subjective, and I won't go deep into that. As a former C# developer, I like the idea of a sound language. As a longtime JavaScript developer and previously a PHP developer, I like to have more freedom and I can get around how JavaScript handles some behaviors. TypeScript is in the middle; Flow is more on one side. In the end, both help developers in some way to be more protected than with Vanilla JavaScript. To me, they both win in that category, and it wasn't a criterion that has a significant impact to lean to one or the other.

TypeScript is the precursor of a superset of JavaScript and brought the notion of the definition file. A definition file allows having types on libraries written in JavaScript. Flow has the same concept but in a different format, which makes them incompatible, and they never did a conversion to leverage TypeScript collection. TypeScript started using two different ways to store the definition file and ended up storing them with NPM instead of relying on a custom tool. Facebook decided to go with a custom tool. TypeScript has 4 153 definition files, and this doesn't count definition files bundled directly in an official JavaScript package. Flow has 382. In mid-2017, getting a definition file for JQuery-UI (250k download per month) or Redux-Thunk (1.7 million downloads per month) is not a problem with TypeScript, but it was unavailable with Flow. This is not a big problem if you are using libraries that Flow supports and is not a big deal if you do not need to have types for a third party. Flow could be used to check your code without having Intellisense for codes outside your project. Nevertheless, it is worth mentioning that TypeScript offers more in that aspect and may be more appealing for someone who enjoys having code completion and IntelliSense when coding for custom code as well as code written by someone else.

A small detail about definition files is that Microsoft offers a "pull request mechanism" for missing definition files as well as accept a pull request on GitHub. Flow also accepts pull requests from contributors outside Facebook, but I haven't found a mechanism to request a library file to Facebook. In the end, if you choose TypeScript, you will have all your definition files under the common NPM directory node_module. With Flow, it will be in a folder named flow-typed. It is not a big difference and doesn't change anything in the balance. If I can bring up my personal point of view, I would say that I like that Microsoft went with the existing and well-known tool NPM and went away from their initial design. Even if it took them three iterations to achieve that goal, it's now in a place where JavaScript developers know, using a tool that is known and doesn't depend on a homemade solution. This had a big impact on the team and me. Being able to use a well-known tool like NPM to reach thousands of types gave us an edge to jump on third parties that we do not know all signatures or potential members by heart. It is something that we thought was a significant factor in our final decision. Again, it all depends on your needs.

Both projects are open source and hosted on GitHub. They differ in terms of license: BSD-3 for Flow, and Apache2 for TypeScript. I am not a license expert, but from what I know, both are fine. The main difference is the language used. While being opensource is great, being able to understand the code is what makes opensource greater. The main point of being open source is to have access to the source code in case something needs to be changed. Another point is to get contributions outside the main organization, as well as to have a transparent channel to bring ideas and issues through. TypeScript is ahead of Flow in about all these particular points. TypeScript source code is easier to read by TypeScript developers because it's written in 100% TypeScript. Flow is written in OCaml. We do not exactly know the lifespan of each of these products, technologies are changing fast, and both of them may stop being developed at some point. For huge software, this might be an argument in favor of TypeScript, since if ever they need to do a fix in TypeScript source code years from now, they will be able to do it more easily than they would in OCaml code. However, this is an edge case, and most people won't mind, and that is understandable. Still, I think it's more a positive aspect than a negative one for TypeScript.

Let's bring some metrics to both open source projects as of March 2018.

Flow has 45 branches; TS has 282.
Flow has 460 contributors; TS has 277.
Flow has 95 releases; TS has 61 (2 months).
Flow had 17 new pull requests last month; TS had 62.
Flow closed 1 232 pull requests; TS closed 6 223.
Flow has 1 305 forks; TS has 4 617.
Flow has 15 619 stars; TS has 31 650.

That's great. But what can we get from these numbers? I am not an expert on open source projects, but I can only see that there is more activity around TypeScript. The number of contributors and releases are in favor of Flow. That said, the number of contributors is significant only if they are all active. The number of releases is also subjective since TypeScript's cadence is every two months; Flow seems to be faster. Does that mean Flow is better? This is subjective since a balance between stability and new features is always at play. TypeScript has more forks and more stars than Flow. Again, what it really means is that people are more interested, hence follow the project more and maybe get the code. Does it mean TypeScript is better? I don't think so. The metric that I am most interested in is the number of pull requests. It's a good indicator that features and bug fixes are coming in. Both Facebook and Microsoft have employees contributing to the code. TypeScript has more than ten times the number of features/fixes coming in than Flow. So, on the open source aspect, TypeScript is one step ahead because of the language used to build it.

Here is a comparison on who is at the head of these two projects. TypeScript is managed by Anders Hejlsberg, creator of Turbo Pascal, Delphi, C# and now TypeScript. Hejlsberg graduated in the '80s, has received many awards in his career, and he is the person who committed the most on GitHub on that project. Flow commits are led by Marshall Roch [11] by a proportion of twice as the next biggest contributor from the second developer on Flow. I assume that he is in charge of Flow (I might be wrong). Roch graduated in 2009 from Carnegie Mellon University and has been working at Facebook for seven years. While this might not be a game-changer, it's also a point for TypeScript. The experience behind the lead of the project is a positive for TypeScript. Flow has the advantage of having fresh eyes on new technologies, hence still not bad. In the end, both projects are not driven by a single man but by a group of people and are simply influenced by the spirit the leaders project.

Visual Studio Code is the preferred language for TypeScript, but they offer a variety of plugins for many IDEs. TypeScript and Flow have the same kind of architecture that lets external programs communicate with the "local server" to get analyzed for type check. Here is the list of supported IDEs for TypeScript:

- alm.tools
- Atom
- CATS
- Eclipse
- Emacs
- NeoVim
- NetBeans
- Notepad++
- Sublime Text
- Vim
- Visual Studio
- Visual Studio Code (VSCode)
- WebStorm

Here is the list of supported IDEs for Flow:

- Visual Studio Code (VSCode)
- Atom
- Nuclide
- Sublime Text

- Vim
- Emacs
- WebStorm

Beyond the support of IDE, there is the experience of the type checker within the IDE. During this comparison, I used Visual Studio Code (VSCode), the editor I use to work on a variety of languages. Integration with TypeScript is seamless; integration with Flow requires an extension. This is how VSCode worked (1 plugin per language) and it installed flawlessly as well. When starting to convert, I added a comment at the top of each JavaScript file to have Flow catch up on verification. I noticed that when fixing issues, it could take between 2 to 5 seconds to have the error removed from the editor. Flow confirms that VSCode lacks the on-the-fly linting and validates only on save, which is also a limitation on the Nuclide editor that Facebook built. Both languages have a suggestion when importing custom type which simplifies the writing of the import. However, Visual Studio Code allows for TypeScript to write the code and detect the missing type, and auto-suggests which import to bring to the top of the file for you. This is a neat feature that didn't trigger while writing with Flow. This might be a limitation of the VSCode plugin. Again, this might not be a big deal, unless you love one IDE and it is not on the list of one or the other. Being used to having TypeScript jump to help me right when I type is also something I was missing with Flow in VSCode. TypeScript covers more IDE, but both are pretty similar in terms of being the most popular ones in web development these days. If I had to declare a winner, I would say TypeScript, but with a marginal gain since it supports more IDEs. It wasn't a decisive point for me or the team since the IDEs we use were covered.

What about if you have a problem and you need an answer? This will happen, and it's interesting to see what both offer. Most developers will use StackOverflow to write a question to get an answer or will search the Internet and stumble at StackOverflow. If we look at StackOverflow, we can see that Flow has 1 213 questions and TypeScript has 48 389. TypeScript is more active, but we have to put in perspective that people are asking questions about TypeScript the type checker, as well as TypeScript the transpiler. It would be fairer to say that Babel + Flow count would be more comparable. I'll come back about TypeScript being more than just a type checker in an instant.

About the potential code on the Internet, there are less examples in Flow. For example, the well-known TodoMvc has an example with TypeScript and React, TypeScript and Angular, TypeScript and Backbone, but none with Flow. The official documentation is detailed in both official websites. It is very clear with examples that both offer interactive online console where you can drop code and test this one. In the end, TypeScript has a slight advantage. It might be because I was hitting lots of garbage while trying to search "flow" + my keywords, but even with "Facebook flow" or "flow js" it wasn't getting better. I can barely find small projects or websites with good examples with Flow. I found more with TypeScript. However, in both cases, JavaScript's examples are way higher than the two type checkers we are evaluating.

During my evaluation of TypeScript versus Flow, I immediately realized that a major difference between the two was that one was doing more than the other. TypeScript is not just a type checker; it's a transpiler. Flow is a type checker, and that's it. What is the advantage of Flow? The advantage is that you can use whatever you want for transpiling. To be honest, it means that you will need BabelJs. BabelJs has the advantage over TypeScript in that you can cherry-pick plugins and presets you want. TypeScript allows you to enable and disable features, but you are limited to the features they release. In the end, BabelJs is very popular and gives more flexibility. TypeScript is simpler to install and compatibility (or configuration) is a breeze. I migrated one of my small projects, which is a React project. Here is the TypeScript configuration followed by the BabelJs and Flow configuration. It has more boilerplate. TypeScript offers stage 2 and up features from ECMAScript because their philosophy is to have all released features backward-compatible (which is true since version 1.0). Earlier stage ECMAScript features are more prone to die or change signatures. With Babel, you can decide at which stage you want to subscribe. This freedom has a cost. TypeScript brings simplicity at the cost of being less cutting edge. But what does it mean at the end? If we look at all of ECMAScript

2016 features, Babel supports 40% of them, TypeScript 36%. In the end, it's only two features different. It's also interesting to note that BabelJs may support features that Flow doesn't. This doesn't occur with TypeScript since they are in symbiosis. For example, Flow doesn't support decorator, but BabelJs and TypeScript do.

CHAPTER 2: CONFIGURATION

TypeScript is flexible in how it can transpile TypeScript to JavaScript. This chapter approaches TypeScript's configurations with a pragmatic view as well as some good practices. The TypeScript transpiler receives its configuration by command line or by consuming a configuration file. The latter is the normal way to handle configuration since it is an official way to avoid repeating configuration between transpilation. Every potential configuration option is available with both methods. Hence, the choice is really for your convenience. TypeScript transpiler is an executable that can be invoked directly from command line or by the IDE. There are existing wrappers for Gulp or Grunt, but at the end, TypeScript executable is always the one running. The Gulp and Grunt wrappers send options specified in the TypeScript transpiler. For Webpack, it executes the command line directly. The direct communication brings the advantage of not relying on a middle-tier when an update of TypeScript's options emerges.

Before going through the list of configurations, it might be interesting to note that the name of the executable that transpiles TypeScript is "tsc." This one is available by NPM. The positive consequence is the simplicity of installing TypeScript with a single line. NPM requires the installation of Node.js.

```
npm install -g typescript
```

While you can use the command line "tsc" most of the time, TypeScript has other ways to work out transpilation. TypeScript architecture has a standalone server named "tsserver" which is used by IDE. It is NodeJS that allows communicating via a JSON protocol. There is also a compiler API available, which is not yet stable, which allows having a basic compiler in TypeScript to build TypeScript. Regardless of these options, the command line interface is the most commonly used for the developer and the option we will use the most in this book.

2.1 TSCONFIG

The configuration of your project is not something you change often, but it needs to remain the same on every developer compute as well during the continuous deployment pipeline you are following. Fortunately, TypeScript has a configuration file that you can have in your code repository that will follow along at every step that requires compilation.

The first thing to know is that by default the name of the configuration is "tsconfig.json" and is located at the root of the TypeScript project. If you invoke the compiler by executing "tsc" without any parameter, it will search a "tsconfig.json" file from the current directory. If it cannot find it, it will go to the parent directory and move up until it finds the file or it reaches the root of your hard drive. Another way to have TypeScript find the configuration file is by providing the parameter "-p" to specify a file name. The argument can be a file name if the file is in the actual directory or can contain a full path. Any file with the extension "json" is interpretable by the command line. Finally, TypeScript can generate a minimal configuration file by using "tsc --init."

There is a lot of possible configurations, and I'll cover the most likely to occur in your project in this section. The file is a JSON file, and under the property under "compilerOptions" resides the core of the configuration.

2.1.1 OUTDIR

The first and foremost configuration concern is where we want to output the JavaScript file produced by TypeScript. Without this configuration, TypeScript transpiles the file directly next to the original files. This causes two issues. The first one is that it creates a messy development environment where the working files mingle with the output files. The second is that it's harder to package for deployment without bringing the TypeScript source files with the JavaScript. It requires additional configuration to whitelist only specific extensions, like only ".js" and ".jsx" and blacklist TypeScript extension ".ts" and ".tsx." To avoid this situation, specifying "outDir" is a good practice. Usually, the "outDir" will set the file in a "build" directory. This root level directory, if not present, is created by TypeScript, and offers a great separation. A separated folder not only allows to easily package at publishing stage of the development but also allows to easily clean up generated files. Again, it's possible to clean up with compiled JavaScript files along with TypeScript using command lines for specific file extensions, but it is again more cumbersome. A good advice is to mark the build directory to ignore for your source control to avoid cluttering the repository. Ignoring the build folder increases the speed of fetching files from the remote repository. A second advice is to configure TypeScript compiler to avoid analyzing the output folder. We will see this configuration soon.

2.1.2 MODULE

The second inevitable configuration is what type of module loader it will follow once you have the code compiled. For example, Node.js usually uses "CommonJS" while web application uses "require.js". As you can see, TypeScript is indifferent about having a synchronous or asynchronous module loader. It only needs to know to be able to produce the right nomenclature between your files. TypeScript can generate many types like CommonJS, AMD, System, UMD, ES6, ES2015, and ESNext. A common pattern is to use CommonJS and Webpack to bundle all the files together for web application instead of Require.js. It allows to bundle and avoid several calls to the backend.

2.1.3 MODULE RESOLUTION

Now that we have configured how JavaScript writes the import and export of modules, we need to tell TypeScript how to navigate in the file structure to find these modules. The option "moduleResolution" is mainly interested in specifying the discovery of modules. There are two options: node or classic. Node is one of the most popular, and classic came in earlier along with TypeScript. I won't go into deep detail, but the difference is how TypeScript looks for files when importing them. For example, with the classic way, if you want to import "file1", it can look at the current directory, and if not found, look at the parent and so on. With the node approach, it will also try the current directory but then will look at the package.json to see under "types" if the module has a custom path and then move to find under directory "file1" if a file named "index.ts" exists.

2.1.4 TARGET

As we already mentioned, TypeScript lets you decide in which version of ECMAScript you want to produce your JavaScript. The ECMAScript preference is set using the "target" configuration. The default value is ES3, but you can select ES5, ES6/ES2015, ES2016, ES2017, or ESNext. A quick remark: TypeScript offers features at stage 2 and beyond from ECMAScript because their philosophy is to have all released features backward-compatible (which is true since version 1.0). Earlier stage ECMAScript features are more prone not to see the light or are more susceptible to change the signature. The target is an important configuration because it allows supporting of older browsers. Deploying JavaScript with a recent ECMAScript on an old browser will fail at runtime because it cannot interpret recent commands. However, with the same TypeScript code base, you can use modern syntax and features and have TypeScript transpiling into a comprehensive JavaScript code for the target selected. For example, you can use the concept of "class" in your TypeScript and target ES3. The result is a JavaScript constructed with function and prototype instead of using a more recent approach of a JavaScript class possible with ES6. Why bother to target higher specification of ECMAScript if TypeScript can transpile to something functional? Simply because modern features are more performant and adapted for the current state of the web.

2.1.5 LIB

TypeScript uses stable features regardless of the target. But what about using specific APIs that are not part of the standard? Specific APIs can be exploited by using the option "lib". Under the hood, the compile includes additional files that contain the logic of these APIs. At design time, TypeScript understands this by looking at definition files that describe the signatures and types of add-ons. For example, you can specify to include "DOM" which will bring HTML DOM manipulation to TypeScript. Why is it not part of the default TypeScript? Because you may create TypeScript code for a non-web project; for instance, a Node.js project that doesn't need to carry the burden of a web library. Sometimes, you will see that the target is "ES5" and that the lib is set to "ES6". The discrepancy between the two ECMAScript means that you can use ES6 features but it will transpile the code into a compatible JavaScript to support ES5, hence polyfill features that are not available. Lib is about before TypeScript outputs the file; target is about the format it outputs. The last example is that you can target ES3 and specify "ES2015.Promise" in the lib. The use of the promise lib means that you can write code in TypeScript using Promise and that TypeScript will figure out how to create JavaScript that can do asynchronous code for ECMAScript 3. A caveat of libs is that when specifying only a specific lib under the lib array in the configuration, you might end up with a bad surprise. Primitive types can stop being recognized by TypeScript. The reason is that once you specify a specific lib, TypeScript stops providing the default ones and hence you must specify all of them. For example, if you desire to use something particular of "es2017.object", specifying only this entry would cause an issue with primitive. However, specifying "dom" as well as "es2017" with the "es2017.object" would work perfectly.

2.1.6 DOWN-LEVEL ITERATION

The Boolean option "downlevelIteration" works in pair with the "target" option. The option aims for iteration solely to support available feature that is only available in ECMAScript 6. By setting the value to "true", the prior versions of ES6 can iterate seamlessly and behave like ES6. When using a target of 6 and above, iteration is already at the latest version, and the flag is elective.

2.1.7 IMPORT HELPERS

The Boolean option "importHelpers" optimizes the size of the generated JavaScript. Depending on the quantity of polyfills and how many times a project uses them, the size of the output can increase drastically. The "importHelpers" brings helper functions instead of declaring many identical polyfills. However, if many files need to use those helper functions, it results in the creation of an overall bigger outputted JavaScript. The reason is that each time a feature needs a polyfill, it will add the polyfill instead of reusing the compatible stubs. A better approach would be to use any imported module and to bring a single instance of the required functions. Reusability is what importHelper is doing by importing module helpers from "tslib." In fact, the mechanism is leveraging an NPM package named "tslib." As a developer, it means that you are required to install the "tslib" package manually if setting the compiler option to true.

2.1.8 SOURCE MAP

TypeScript allows you not only to create a JavaScript file but also to generate a source map file by specifying "sourceMap" to true. The option is likely to be set to true if you want to simplify your debugging session. SourceMap shows TypeScript files in the developer tool source instead of in the generated JavaScript. The readability increases and breakpoints can be set and executed directly into the TypeScript file. You will be able to inspect variables, step into functions, etc. The source map allows you to link the source code and the generated code.

2.1.9 ALLOWJS

The Boolean configuration "allowJs" is useful if you need to migrate a project from JavaScript to TypeScript. This option tells TypeScript how to interpret JavaScript files. That is right; TypeScript can generate JavaScript from JavaScript. TypeScript can transform a JavaScript file to be compatible with the desired target, but also to make some basic syntax errors. In the case of a project with JavaScript and TypeScript, this option becomes handy. Not only is it useful because the JavaScript files will be in the output directory amongst the transpiled TypeScript files output but it also does minor syntax checks. This option is not useful if you start a new project without JavaScript. However, it's a crucial addition to the compiler to break an entry barrier for people who have a legacy application but still want to bring TypeScript into play.

2.1.10 ROOTDIR

The "rootDir" option lets you specify the root directory where the transpiler should look for files. For example, if you have a project that has all its source under "src," you can set the "rootDir" to "src." "rootDir" is important if you have several directories that don't have any relation with TypeScript.

2.1.11 STRICT

TypeScript lets you tune up and down how strict it can apply rules. Some of them should be turned on right from the start of a new project, but it can be too restrictive for an existing project. The first option is called "noImplicitAny." This option allows TypeScript to return an error at transpilation time anytime it finds a variable of "any" type. We will talk about "any" later in this book, but as good practice, it's better to use "let" or "const". "noImplicitReturns" is also an option that forces specifying a return type on all your functions. The option ensures you are returning the specified type from the function's signature. Without it, you may assume that any line of code in a function can return any specific type and even return "void" if nothing explicitly returned. By specifying an explicit return type in the signature, you cannot fall into the trap of returning something unexpected which can occur when TypeScript infers the return type. "noImplicitThis" is a third option that helps to have the right reference on this. "This" can be a pitfall when mixing function and arrow function. The last option you want to turn on around strict validation is "strickNullCheck" which will not have null or undefined set of specific type as a number. The scope of potential values for a specific type is crucial to know what is set into the variable. With the check enabled, it's 100% reliable to know if a specific variable is defined. In case we want to allow an actual type and potentially null or undefined, it is also possible by explicitly specifying the three desired types. We will see the syntax later.

TypeScript can be tuned to be stricter, which increases the type safety without having to specify compiler options manually. This compiler option got introduced in TypeScript 2.3 in four different knobs that can be turned on or off. By default, everything is turned on, which makes TypeScript safer by default. Using "strict" brings the advantage of having future potential strict options incorporated into the compiler and benefit from it by default.

The strict options check null, do not allow implicit "any", do not allow implicit "this", and are to be always strict. To have everything turned on, you can specify the option "strict" in the "tsconfig.json" file. To turn on specific strict options, you need to write the option name in the configuration file and set it to true as well. It's possible to combine; for example, setting everything to true by setting "strict" to true and a specific option to false.

The "AlwaysStrict" option will parse TypeScript in strict mode and will add "use strict" in each JavaScript file. The three other options have already been discussed in the compiler option and are not new. The novelty is the capability to have everything on by default and to turn on and off a batch of them.

Finally, TypeScript with its version 2.7 brings more rigidity around class properties. For many years, it was possible to define class properties without initializing them at the declaration level, neither in the constructor. Before 2.7, the only difference between an optional and a non-optional class property was that optional could receive the value of undefined, while the other one was undefined until a value was set. After initialized, the non-optional protects the field to receive undefined. However, the case of declaring and not defining the value makes TypeScript less valuable by creating confusion. The nomenclature indicates that a field cannot be undefined but the missing initialization creates a limbo where the value is something not allowed. TypeScript 2.7 brings a new compiler flag: "strictPropertyInitialization". This new strict flag indicates to TypeScript that any class property must initialize the field at the declaration time or inside the constructor of the class.

Let's see an example of that compile prior to the adoption of "strictPropertyInitialization" or if this flag is set to false. The following code shows three properties. The "m1" is initialized in the constructor. The "m2" is initialized at declaration. The "m3" is initialized by a call to a method from the constructor. The last example works only without the flag set to true.

```
class C {
   private m1: number;
   private m2: string = "2";
   private m3: boolean;

   public constructor() {
      this.m1 = 1;
      this.init();
   }
   private init():void {
      this.m3 = true;
   }
}
```

The problem with initializing in a method is the lack of guarantee of invocation. The call to the method might be immediate or might be under a condition that makes it not initialize or to partially initialize its properties. TypeScript can perform a deeper analysis if it concentrates on each field and under a single method -- the constructor.

Let's examine a second example where the compiler catches a missing initialization.

```
class C2 {
   private m1: number;
   private m2: string = "2";
   private m3: boolean;

   public constructor(b: boolean) {
      this.m1 = 1;
      if (b) {
         this.m3 = true;
      }
   }
}
```

The second example initializes the field "m3" but not in every code path. TypeScript detects that the field might not be initialized, hence doesn't compile. An important detail is the flag enters in action when TypeScript configures the "strictNullChecks" to true. Otherwise, TypeScript accepts undefined without mentioning optional. The combination of strict flags "strictNullChecks" and "strictPropertyInitialization" works hand in hand to reduce potential undesired undefined value for field and doesn't mention the possibility of undefined.

2.1.12 EXCLUDE

There are many other options under the "compilerOptions," property, but the discussed ones are the principal. A property parallel to the "compilerOptions" in the configuration file is the "exclude" option. In almost every project, this option is required. This option lets you specify an array of the folder's paths that TypeScript will preclude. Most of the time, you will see "node_modules" and "build" on that list.

2.1.13 TYPES

Another option called "types" is available under "compilerOptions". "types" is an array of TypeScript's definition file name read by the compiler. This option indicates to TypeScript to look for specific definition files instead of looking for declaration files under the node_modules/@types/ folder. This is the way to work with the global declaration. As a best practice, you should not rely on automatic inclusion from this property and should import all types you are using without a global declaration. For example, instead of using "import MyFile", you should do "import class1 from ../Folder1/MyFile" for the module you coded and relied on the default node_modules for third-party libraries. By leaving this property alone when importing a class without using a relative path, TypeScript will look at the node_module/@types/ folder. The "types" work with the "typeRoots". TypeScript finds libraries specified by "types" under "typeRoots". You can see the default configuration of "typeRoots" to be node_modules/@types/.

TypeScript has two compiler's options that help developers when developing. The first one is the "watch" option. The watch will automatically transpile the code when a file changes. Version 2.6 brings a narrower transpilation which focuses on the changed module instead of compiling the whole project. A target compilation is also present when TypeScript performs real-time validation in the IDE. The second compiler option is "pretty" which change the display of errors. Here is an example with and without "pretty."

```
src/comparison4.ts(1,7): error TS2451: Cannot redeclare block-scoped variable 'x'.
src/declarationScope.ts(1,5): error TS2451: Cannot redeclare block-scoped variable 'x'.
src/declarationScope.ts(2,5): error TS2451: Cannot redeclare block-scoped variable 'x'.
```

```
src/stringType.ts:2:5 - error TS2451: Cannot redeclare block-scoped variable 'x'.

2 let x = "this is a string with the value " + w;
      ~
```

2.1.14 UNUSED

TypeScript can help in reducing dead code. It's possible to turn on "noUnusedLocals" and "noUnusedParameters." The former flags as an error any value that is not being read, and the latter flags a parameter not consumed by its function. The local checks will raise an error if a statement assigns a value to a variable without having any subsequent line that read it. In the code below, the "p2" parameter is an error and can be removed. The first line of the function is also an error because it doesn't do anything with the variable.

```
function notUsedFunction(p1: number, p2: number): void {
   const unusedVariable = p1 + 100;
   console.log("The parameter 1 value is " + p1);
}
```

2.2 MULTIPLE CONFIGURATION

As we saw in the previous section, the configuration file can contain a lot of crucial information. However, what if you want to have multiple configurations? The system lets your configuration spread over multiple files. There is a property named “extends” located at the same level of “compilerOptions” which accepts a string that specifies a file name (without an extension). Extending means that you can have a base file (e.g., base.json) that is used by multiple configuration files. For example, tsconfig.json and tsconfig.test.json can extend base.json. In both files, in tsconfig.json and in tsconfig.test.json, you will see an entry: “extends”: “./base.”

As you may imagine, a configuration overlap may happen if a configuration is written in multiple levels of hierarchy. To resolve any conflict, TypeScript works by priority from the extends file and then by the extended one. For example, the first set of rules applied is the base file, “base.json” in our example, followed by the one that extends (e.g. “tsconfig.json”). The priority logic allows having the extended one to override instruction if required.

In this chapter, we learned a few crucial and high-likelihood used TypeScript compiler’s configurations. We also tiptoe at the conundrum of dividing configuration with inheritance. We can thank the Angular team that had many repeated configurations and provided a good use case for the final solution. In the next chapter, we will tackle many topics around variables as an introduction to TypeScript’s language features.

CHAPTER 3: VARIABLES: THE BASIS

This chapter starts our journey about TypeScript the language, and it dives into the basis. We will initially start with how to declare variables, the scope in which they can operate, and see all primitive types.

3.1 DECLARATION

There are a few ways to declare variables but overall funneled down to two: "let" and "const." The "var" declaration and "declare" also exist but are more rarely used.

```
let x = "variable x is a string";
const y = 1;
var z = "this is a string but the scope is not block scoped";
```

3.1.1 VAR

Let's get started with "var." The usage of "var" has been the way to define variable since the inception of JavaScript until ECMAScript2015 when "let" and "const" arrived, fixing drawbacks perpetuated in previous ECMAScript versions. The problem with "var" is that it requires particular attention to know what is happening. In many modern languages, declaring a variable is as simple as being alive in the scope where this one was defined. For example, a variable declared in a conditional statement is only available inside the conditional statement – not before or after. One "var" issue is that the declaration position of a variable makes it not predictable. The variable with "var" is function-scoped when declared inside a function, but global-scoped when declared outside of a function. Also, "var" lets you define more than once the same variable which overrides the initial declaration or initialization.

```
function varFunction(){
  var x = "111";
  if(true){
    var x = 999;
  }
  console.log(x); // 999
}
varFunction();
```

3.1.2 LET

The keyword "let" comes to the rescue by setting the lifespan of the variable at the block where it was declared. A scoped variable lifespan is the normal behavior of declaration mentioned earlier in many languages. Curly braces determine a block. For example, if you declare a variable with "let" within an "if" statement, the variable will not be accessible as soon as the execution leaves the "if." The rule is true for a function, a loop, and a class. About loop, if you are defining a "for" loop and you define the iterative "i", this one should use "let" which allows modifying its values while being only available for the loop.

```
function letFunction(){
  let x = "111";
  if(true){
    let x = 999;
  }
  console.log(x); // "111"
}
letFunction();
```

3.1.3 CONST

The keyword "const", for constant, is similar to "let" about the scope of its lifespan. However, this one has the restriction of being initialized only once: in its declaration. The restriction is powerful because it not only syntactically indicates that the purpose is not to change its value, but TypeScript will also ensure that no value can be set. It's important to understand that if you have a constant object, the value of the object can change. However, no assignation to the variable is authorized. For example, you declare and initialize a variable that holds the current user of your application to a constant. You won't be able to assign the current user to any other user. However, you can set its name if a public member is available. You will be very surprised that most variable can be constant.

```
function constFunction(){
  const x = "111";
  x = "this won't compile"; // This won't compile!
  if(true){
    const x = 999;
  }
  console.log(x); // "111"
}
constFunction();
```

3.1.3 HOISTING

Before moving on, let's talk about the concept of "hoisting." The concept is a quirk of JavaScript that brings all declaration with "var" at the top of the function (or global scope if declared outside a function). The particularity does not affect "let" or "const." It means that if you are using "var" you can use the variable and declare it later and the code will still work. It's a bad practice that makes the code hard to follow. The ambiguity is solved by "let" and "const" which do not allow using a variable not declared before using it.

```
x = "not declared before assignation";
var x = "declared after assignation and all fine"; // Will be hoisted above

y = "not declared before assignation"; // Doesn't compile
let y = "The line before forbid this line";;

z = "not declared before assignation"; // Doesn't compile
const z = "The line before forbid this line";
```

3.1.4 DECLARE

The keyword "declare" can be used before one of the previous three declaration types (var, let, const). As the name suggests, it declares to TypeScript that the variable is somewhere but not saying where. This is not used frequently, but can be used if you need to tell the transpiler that the variable is present, just not in the current project (or loaded module), hence not visible. The official jargon is "ambient declaration." If you are working with JavaScript and that there is no definition file, you may want to use "declare" since you know that you will import the code and that the variable will be present. Unfortunately, you will lose all Intellisense since "declare" doesn't have type provided.

```
declare let variableDefinedSomewhereElse: any;
let newVariable = variableDefinedSomewhereElse + 1;
```

3.2 SCOPE

We briefly encounter the concept of scope when exposing the three declaration types. We saw that "var" scope is broader than its two counterparts, which are more restrained. However, there are some other cases with a scope with "let" and "const."

3.2.1 SHADOWING

The first case is called "shadowing." Shadowing is where you are using an imbricated scope with the same variable in the outer scope and inner scope; for example, if you have two loops and both of them are using the variable "i." It will work because TypeScript is smart enough to understand that both declarations are for two different variables. However, it's confusing and susceptible to error, hence not recommended even if the code will transpile without a problem.

```
function f1(i: number) {
  console.log("Parameter value", i);
  let i: number = 10; // Shadow #1
  console.log("Variable value", i);
  for (let i = 100; i < 101; i++) { // Shadow #2
    console.log("For-statement value", i);
    for (let i = 200; i < 201; i++) { // Shadow #3
      console.log("For-statement value 2", i);
    }
  }
  console.log("Variable value", i);
}
f1(0);
```

3.2.2 CAPTURING

The second case is called "capturing." Capturing occurs when you have a variable that you define in an inner scope and then use it inside a function that you assign to another scope. During the assignation of the function, the variable defined in the inner scope will be captured, like a snapshot, and when leaving the scope, the function declared before the inner scope will still have the value of the variable.

```
function mainFunction() {
  let innerFunction;
  if (true) {
    // Environment for capturing start here
    let variableCapturedByTheInnerFunction
        = "AvailableToTheInnerFunction";
    innerFunction = function() {
      return variableCapturedByTheInnerFunction;
    }
    // Environment for capturing stop here
  }
  return innerFunction();
}
console.log(mainFunction());
```

3.2.3 ONE DECLARATION

A third case is that in the same scope you can only declare once with the same name a variable with "let" and "const" but you can define as many times as you want with "var."

```
var x = "First time";
var x = "Second time";
let y = "First time"; // Doesn't compile
let y = "ERROR!"; // Doesn't compile
const z = "First time"; // Doesn't compile
const z = "ERROR!"; // Doesn't compile
```

TypeScript is well suited to help you avoid "var" quirks and embrace the use of "let" and "const" to avoid confusion. The compiler highlights every shadowing situation with "var". It is possible to tweak the compiler to generate errors when hoisting or shadowing cases are present.

3.2.4 SWITCH STATEMENT SCOPE

A switch statement requires using curly brackets after the colon and after the break statement. Otherwise, variables defined within the parent scope are shared. This is not a constraint with TypeScript but it is with ECMAScript.

```
function switchFunction(a: number): void {
  switch (a) {
    case 1:
      let variableInCase1 = "test";
      console.log(variableInCase1);
      break;
    case 2:
      let variableInCase1 = "test2"; // Error! Cannot redeclare
      console.log(variableInCase1);
      break;
  }
}
```

The correct form is with a curly bracket to create a scope.

```
function switchFunction(a: number): void {
  switch (a) {
    case 1: {
      let variableInCase1 = "test";
      console.log(variableInCase1);
      break;
    }
    case 2: {
      let variableInCase1 = "test2"; // Error! Cannot redeclare
      console.log(variableInCase1);
      break;
    }
  }
}
```

3.3 TYPE

Using TypeScript is all about type – it's even in the name of the language. Type allows having a predictable code that defines what kind of data is passed in and out. With type, usage of object's members is no more in the range of assumption. It's clear on what members are accessible at any time since types bring a contract that must be respected. Types self-constraint potential operation and manipulation depend on the nature of the type. In this section of the chapter, we will see all the primitive types as the main type provided with TypeScript, from array to generic to literal and object.

3.4 STRING DECLARATION

The first primitive is the string. A string is any characters. It can be assigned a single quote or double quote. A string content can be a number but will behave as characters if between quotes. Both are accepted; however, the guideline of the TypeScript project uses double quote. By the way, TypeScript is written in TypeScript. There is also the possibility to use the backquote for string interpolation. String interpolation allows templating a string to avoid having to concatenate with the plus sign many strings. It helps to have a cleaner string built. The syntax starts a backquote and writes all strings desired as usual with a single or double quote. The value of a variable is embedded in the string by using the dollar sign followed by a curly brace. The insertion of the name of the variable must follow. The use of an ending curly brace is required, and from there, you can write any other characters until closing the string by using the second backquote. The placeholder is often a variable, but you can insert any TypeScript expression.

```
let w = "Value1";
let x = "this is a string with the value " + w;
let y = 'this is a string with the value ' + w;
let z = `this is a string ${w}`;
```

3.5 STRING MULTIPLE LINES

TypeScript can write strings on multiple lines without requiring the use of the backslash "n" (\n) that is required by JavaScript. This shorthand removes the boilerplate of having to bring many characters by allowing to hit enter to switch line. Similar to string interpolation, it requires the use of backquotes. Inside the backquote, every changed line will be considered as if you were explicitly using the \n. The result of the string interpolation produces multiple strings with backslash "n."

```
let multiline1 = "Line1\n"
+ "Line2\n"
+ "Line3\n";

let multiline2 = `Line1
Line2
Line3`;
```

3.6 STRING TEMPLATE

The last detail about TypeScript and string is that you can call "tagged template." The concept is rarely used but offers a possibility to specify a function before opening a backquote. Each group of string and placeholder defined by the dollar sign and curly braces, as seen before for expression, calls the function. This time, you still provide an expression, but you can have the whole string manipulated by the method (placeholders and string before and after placeholders). Furthermore, the method is reusable! The function provided in the tagged template takes two parameters. The first one will be all string literal in an array, and the second is a list of all placeholders. The string literal is all the text that is not a placeholder. For example, you can have a sentence that contains a few characters and a placeholder followed by some other characters and another placeholder. In front of the string, you transform it into a tagged template by having a tag. The tag is a function you place in front of the backquote. The function first parameter is an array with two items, and a second array with the placeholders. The return of the function must be a string.

```
const number = 84
const number2 = 100;
const endResult = analyzeString `The number is ${number} which is not like
the second number ${number2}`;

// literals:
// [0] "The number is"
// [1] " which is not like the second number "

// placeholders:
// [0] 84
// [1] 100
function analyzeString(literals: TemplateStringsArray, ...placeholders:any[])
{
  let result = "";
  for (let i = 0; i < placeholders.length; i++) {
    result += literals[i];
    result += "*" + placeholders[i] + "*";
  }
  result += literals[literals.length - 1];
  return result;
}
console.log(endResult);
```

3.7 NUMBER

The second most-used primitive is probably the number. TypeScript is a superset of JavaScript, and the number in TypeScript is the number in JavaScript. The openness of JavaScript allows a broad set of numbers. An integer, a signed float or unsigned float is permitted. By default, a number is base 10, but you can assign base 16 (hexadecimal) or base 8 (octal) or base 2 (binary) with the prefix "0x", "0o" and "0b". It's rarely used but possible.

```
const x: number = 10;
const y: number = 0x10;
const z: number = 0o10;
const b:number = 0b10;
console.log("Here is 4 numbers", x,y,z,b);
// Here is 4 numbers 10 16 8 2
```

3.7.1 NUMERIC SEPARATOR

A numeric separator is a feature that simplifies how to write the number. A long number can be hard to read and adding a separator can reduce confusion. When writing a number, you can use the underscore symbol to mark every thousand, for example. There is no rule where to place a group separator other than it must be between two numbers.

```
const numericSeparator1 = 560000067;
const numericSeparator2 = 560_000_067;
const numericSeparator3 = 5_6_0_000_0_6_7;
const numericSeparator4 = Number(5_000);
const numericSeparator5 = Number("5_000"); // Nan
const numericSeparator6 = parseInt("5_000");
const numericSeparator7 =  0xFAB_F00D;
const numericSeparator8 =  0b1111_11111000_11110000_00001100;
```

Numeric separator works with decimal, octal, binary and hexadecimal. It is available from TypeScript 2.7 and in stage 3 with ECMAScript. Meanwhile, TypeScript transforms the separator out during transpilation.

3.8 BOOLEAN

A Boolean value is the most basic primitive in JavaScript, and it remains the same with TypeScript. Boolean restricts the assignation to two values: true and false. Only the lowercase format is accepted. You cannot assign the value 0 or 1, neither the true or false in cases other than lower case. You can reverse a Boolean value by assigning the same value with an exclamation point before.

```
let b: boolean = true;
let reverse = !b;
let isEqual: boolean = 1 > 0;
```

3.9 ANY

You must avoid as much as possible the "any" type, principally because it can hold any value and by consequence doesn't enforce any protection. If you are integrating an existing JavaScript project with TypeScript, every variable will be by default set to "any" until they are defined. It is also the case with a value coming from an Ajax response in JSON format. Every "any" variable will let you assign any value but also could invoke any function. The danger is that the function may not be available. For example, you may set a variable with a number value that calls for an array of function ".length" which will transpile, but raise a runtime exception because a number doesn't have a length in the browser, and undefined when running under NodeJs.

```
let x: any = "string";
x = true;
x = { title: "Object with a string member" };
x = [1, 2, 3];
x = 1;
console.log(x.length); // Undefined
console.log(x.asd);    // Undefined
```

3.10 ARRAY

Array in TypeScript is exactly like in JavaScript in terms of features. The difference is that TypeScript assigns a type to the list. The syntax uses the square brackets with the actual type before the brackets and after the colon. You can initialize the list to be empty by equaling the variable to square brackets. An array can use one or many unions to allow multiple types. Union's details will be discussed later. At that stage, the detail to remember is with multiple types to wrap the union with parentheses. Using multiple types will require you to evaluate what is the type of each value before using an individual item of the array. The reason is that variable's operations are type-dependent. An equivalence syntax is to use the generic "Array<T>." Both are the same.

```
let a: number[] = [1, 2, 3];
let b: (number | boolean)[] = [1, true, 3];
let c: Array<number> = [1, 2, 3];
```

3.11 NULL AND UNDEFINED

A variable declared but not initialized is undefined. Undefined is different from the similar type null. In both cases, an assignation can set undefine or null to a variable explicitly. However, only undefined is a natural default choice.

TypeScript must be tuned up in strictness to dissociate the possibility of assigning null or undefined to every type. TypeScript must set the option "strictNullChecks" at true to block the possibility of implicit null and undefined to all types (available since TypeScript 2.0). Doing so forces developers to use the question mark to define the variable as optional which allow undefined. A nullable number is underneath two types. Dual type (or more) is possible with a union. The union uses the pipe character between the main type (for example, a number) and null.

The union of a type and undefined makes the type optional. The question mark syntax or union with undefined produces the same result with a minor subtilty. The question mark is more succinct but also doesn't allow a non-undefined parameter to follow in a function signature.

```
function function1(a:number|undefined, b:number){
}

function function2(a?:number, b:number){
    // Doesn't compile because a is using optional ? and b is not undefined
}
```

A good practice is to avoid using null as much as possible and relying on undefined. The reason is to avoid having to handle undefined and null as well as the actual type. The justification for choosing undefined instead of null is because of the natural tendency of JavaScript to lean toward undefined. Members in a class set to a single type (without a union) cannot be null or undefined explicitly but will be undefined until initialized. The time window between the declaration at the class level and the initialization by the constructor or until it is assigned creates a state where the variable is undefined. A variable can be undefined regardless of the official type.

```
let aNumber: number = 2; // cannot be undefined
aNumber = undefined;  // "strictNullChecks": true => won't compile
function f1(
   p1: null | undefined | number,
   p2: undefined | number,
   p3?: number
){
}
```

There are several use cases where undefined can be handy. A first case is when a function or class doesn't require the variable; for example, an optional parameter or defined members but not used all the time.

A second case is for optional data. Data can be optional and handled with a default behavior or value when the code needs to access the value of the variable. Often, third-party libraries provide default values but let users customize function calls. In that case, the third-party code checks to see if the option is defined (not-undefined) and use it. Otherwise, if undefined, it will use the default value.

A third case is where data are pulled from external sources. The variable starts undefined until the data arrives from the external sources.

Undefined and optional transpile into the same code as if nothing were assigned to the variable. The reason is that JavaScript is not aware of the concept.

3.12 VOID

Void means nothing. However, undefined can be assigned to void. The operation of setting undefined to void is not useful per se. However, a function that returns nothing should be marked with the void reserved keyword. Not marking the function to void implicitly sets the return to "any." The issue of not marking the function with "void" when expecting nothing is that it can involve someone returning a value since "any" means allowing everything. By setting to void, trying to return anything other than undefined will result in a compilation error. Also, by default, returning "any" means that someone could misuse the result of the function. A misuse arrives when an invocation from the result by using a function that doesn't exist occur at runtime and raise an error. It is not recommended to use "any" or no type and recommended to use void to avoid any unnoticed change in behavior.

Concerning functions returning undefined, it becomes interesting when we analyze the return of a void function. A function with a signature that returns void can still assign its return value to a variable. Comparing the variable against undefined shows that the value is undefined. This might be surprising since the type "void" is expected.

```
function voidFunction(): void {
}

if (voidFunction() === undefined) {
  console.log("undefined");
}
```

3.13 NEVER

The type "never" means that nothing occurs. A use case is when a type guard cannot occur or in a situation where the exception is always thrown. There is a difference between void and never. A function that has the explicit return type of "never" won't accept returning "undefined" which is different from a "void" function which allows returning "undefined.

```
function functionThrow(): never {
  throw new Error("This function return never");
}
```

Every TypeScript type is a subtype of "never." Hence, you can return "never" (for example, throwing an exception) when a return type is specified to be void or string but cannot return a string when explicitly marked as never.

TypeScript can benefit from the "never" type by performing an exhaustive check. An exhaustive check verifies that every possibility (for all types in the union or all choices in an enum) is called. The idea is that TypeScript can find unhandled scenario as early as design time but also at compilation time. It works by having a potential path that falls under the "else" condition which returns "never." However, when all type of the union or the enum sways the code to return something than "never" the compiler won't complain. Using never is helpful when code around multiple type value evolves. In the case where an option is added, which occurs when the type gets a new union type or when a new item joins an enum, TypeScript will compute that the function can return "never" and not compile. Since version 2.0, TypeScript can find out if the code has entered in the default case (or "else" case if you are not using the switch statement). For example, in the code below, there is an enum with two items. TypeScript knows that only two cases can occur and the default (else) case cannot occur. This insight of TypeScript is perfect since the function return type only accepts "string" and does not accept "never. If in the future we add a new enum's item, for example, a "ChoiceC" without adding a new case in the switch statement, then the code can call the "unhandledChoice" function which returns "never."

```
enum EnumWithChoices {
  ChoiceA,
  ChoiceB,
}

function functionReturnStringFromEnum(c: EnumWithChoices): string {
  switch (c) {
    case EnumWithChoices.ChoiceA:
      return "A";
    case EnumWithChoices.ChoiceB:
      return "B";
    default:
      return unhandledChoiceFromEnum(c);
  }
}

function unhandledChoiceFromEnum(x: never): never {
  throw new Error("Choice not defined");
}
```

3.14 STRING LITERAL

String literal is a way to define a string but limits the potential value to be used. It's used mostly with the union which allows specifying more than one string value. Imagine that you allow several string's values but want to limit the choice to specific ones. You could use an enumeration, but a string may be more clear or compatible with existing libraries. For example, you may want to limit the value to "north," "south," "east," "west." To create the string literal, define each value separated by the pipe symbol. TypeScript will be smart enough not to compile if it goes outside the defined range. We will see later that with object-oriented overload functions, that string literal can become handy to distinguish between overload when only the value of the string changes. Similarly, it's possible to use numbers to have a set of values. Using multiple defined numbers is convenient if you have a set of values that you accept but not all numbers. For example, if you create a framework where you want to create a view grid system which works on a grid of 12 columns, you may restrict the choice from 1 to 12.

```
type myType = "north" | "south" | "east" | "west";
let x: myType = "north";
```

3.15 SYMBOL

Symbol is a primitive type in ECMAScript 2015 and beyond. TypeScript supports the standard. The equal sign assigns a value to a symbol without the keyword "new" but with parentheses like an object. Symbol's goal is to provide a unique and immutable variable. A symbol can take a parameter with a string value. Defining two symbols with the same parameter will produce a different symbol. In fact, the parameter is just there to help developers when printing out the symbol to the console. It's a way to differentiate them visually. The main difference between a constant and a symbol is that the symbol is unique. With a string constant, someone could pass a string with the same value of the constant and this one would be accepted. However, using a constant symbol, only the same symbol constant would equal. Nothing can coerce a symbol into a string. It means that you cannot add a string to it and expect to have a string.

```
var v1 = "value1";
var v2 = "value1";
if (v1 === v2) {
  console.log("Equal"); // This will print
}
var s1 = Symbol("value1");
var s2 = Symbol("value1");
if (s1 === s2) {
  console.log("Equal"); // This will not print, they are not equal
}
```

An object property can be a symbol. Its assignation uses the symbol between brackets. One subtilty is that property defined with a symbol won't appear in the result of invoking Object.defineProperty or Object.getOwnPropertyNames. To get all properties defined by symbols, you must use getOwnPropertySymbols. If all properties defined are required, the use of Reflect.ownKeys() will be mandated. In the end, the goal is to provide a unique way to define a specific member of the object and avoid a potential collision that a string cannot prevent.

```
const prop1 = Symbol();

const obj = {
   [prop1]: "p1"
};

console.log(obj.prop1); // undefined
console.log(obj[prop1]); // "p1"
```

3.16 TYPEOF

Borrowing the type of other variable is possible by using "typeof." Borrowing type brings at design time protection by allowing to set a type without defining an actual interface or type. For example, you define a variable with a curly braces with some members. There is no actual way to get the schema of the object. However, with "typeof" you can extract the type from the variable. The extraction is true for variable or parameter. Instead of a concrete type, the variable uses "typeof" followed by the name of the variable to borrow the schema. Type aliases are the name given to the technique.

The transposition of the returned type from "typeof" can be in a concrete type by using "type" keyword followed by the name of the type you create by extracting this one from "typeof."

```
let myObject = { name: "test" };
let myOtherObject: typeof myObject; // Borrow type
myOtherObject = { name: "test2" };
type TypeFromTypeOf = typeof myObject; // Borrow
```

TypeScript carries, since version 2.0, something named "control flow analysis" which allows being smarter, depending on how the code behaves with some variables. Control flow analysis is especially useful when a variable can be of multiple types; for example, if a variable is defined to be a number, a string or undefined. TypeScript goes with the most specific type that a statement can provide to give a hint for the actual underlying type. For example, if you check for "undefined," everything after the check will be a string or a number. Thus TypeScript knows that "undefined" cannot be beyond that point and won't complain about checking for "undefined" when accessing members of the variable. Comparing with "typeof" can narrow down types, if needed. The example was using primitives, but the type can be narrowed down to object, array, or any type of aliases or interfaces. It's important to note that "typeof" cannot be used against a class or an interface. We will see how to handle more complex scenarios later.

```
let myObject = { name: "test" };
let myOtherObject: typeof myObject;
myOtherObject = { name: "test2" };
type TypeFromTypeOf = typeof myObject;

function f(param1: number | string | undefined) {
  if (param1 === undefined) {
    console.log("It's undefined");
  } else if (typeof param1 === "number") {
    console.log("It's a number");
  } else if (typeof param1 === "string") {
    console.log("It's a string");
  }
}
```

TypeOf doesn't work as you may expect with class and interface. In both cases, "type of" returns "object." To determine the type of a class, the use of "instanceOf" is required. Further discussion on "instanceOf" will follow. For interface, many strategies exist but it is trickier since there is no runtime equivalence in JavaScript. Interface comparisons will be discussed as well later in this book.

```
class    { private x: string = "val1"; public y: string = "val2"; }
interface InterfaceTypeOf { y: string; }

const classTypeOf = new ClassToUseWithTypeOf();
const interTypeOf: InterfaceTypeOf = { y: "test" };

console.log("Class TypeOf", typeof (classTypeOf)); // object
console.log("Interface TypeOf", typeof (interTypeOf)); // object
```

3.17 GENERIC

Generic brings a possibility to improve reusability by allowing to pass a type to another one. One of the famous examples is a list. With generic, you can define a variable that will be a list of a specific type, let's say numbers. You can develop a list class that will handle any type, and with generic you open the door to let the consumer of your class define what will be in the list without changing the core logic of the list. Generic is not required in JavaScript or even before TypeScript implemented the notion of generic since you can use the loose type "any." The drawback of the "any" is that you cannot restrain the type passed to your class to have a minimal definition and that you will have to cast back for usage once the data is extracted from your class.

```
const a: Array<string> = new Array("abc", "def");
const s: string = a[0]; // No cast required
console.log(s.substr(0,1)); // Access to string members
```

3.17.1 GENERIC CONSTRAINT

With generic, you can specify that the type passed into your generic class must extend a specific interface. Generic allows having code that can rely on minimal code without forcing a specific class. For example, with the list, you do not need to force to have a list of the users. You can create a generic list where the generic type passed must extend a definition which indicates to have a number "id." By extending the generic type, you can do logic on specific members; for example, access "id" regardless of fields not exposed to the generic code.

```
interface MyType {
  id: number;
}
interface AnotherType extends MyType {
}
const arg: AnotherType = { id: 1 };
function genericFunction<T extends MyType>(p1: T) {
}
genericFunction(arg); // This is legit
genericFunction({ id: 123 }); // This is legit
genericFunction("doesn't compile");
```

3.17.2 GENERIC WITH CLASS TYPES

Different patterns can also require instantiating a generic type. Like with type constraint, you can constrain other than with members like to have a constructor. It's possible to use the constructed signature in a construction function to dynamically create a new instance of generic. For example, a function taking "T" as a generic argument can require having its argument of type {new(): T; } and returns T.

```
interface IMyInterfaceWithConstructor<T> {
  new(param: string): T;
}

function createInstance<T>(ctor: IMyInterfaceWithConstructor<T>): T {
  return new ctor("test");
}
```

3.17.3 BEYOND CLASS

Generic is a concept that is not limited to class. It can be used directly on global function or interfaces. You can have a function that takes generic parameters and also returns a generic type.

3.17.4 GENERIC INTERFACE

Inference with generic is possible. If a function takes a parameter of the type "T" and it returns "T" as well, parameter assigned will define the generic type, and the return inferred to type "T." The only exception is that if your function doesn't use the value T, it will return an empty object type.

```
function genericInferred<T>(param:T){
}
genericInferred("str"); // T is of type string by inference
genericInferred<string>("str"); // Same as above, no inference
```

3.17.5 GENERIC COMPARISON

The generic code doesn't allow the use of "typeof" on T, type "new T" or "instanceof" T. The reason is that the transpilation step removes all trace of type. TypeScript transpiles "typeOf" and "instanceOf" operations into JavaScript, and during that step, it erases types. The absence of type at runtime justifies the lack of generic type verification at runtime as well.

3.17.6 GENERIC DEFAULT TYPE

TypeScript allows defining default type for generic, also known as "generic parameter defaults." The syntax is intuitive which is the equal sign of the generic type. The generic type parameter doesn't need to be explicit when an optional value is provided. TypeScript can infer its type.

```
interface MyGenericWithDefault<T = string> {
  myTypeWhichIsStringIfNotSpecified: T;
}
const myGeneric1: MyGenericWithDefault<number>
= { myTypeWhichIsStringIfNotSpecified: 1 };
const myGeneric2: MyGenericWithDefault
= { myTypeWhichIsStringIfNotSpecified: "string" };
```

Like default with function's parameters, default type can only be used after required types. That means that specifying non-default generic type after a specified after a default doesn't compile.

```
interface MyGenericWithDefaults<T = string, Y> {} // Doesn't compile
```

There is a special case with generic and interfaces. Interfaces defined in two different places bring the optional value from one interface into the second one during the merge of the schema. In the following example, three interfaces with three different generic levels. TypeScript merges the interfaces and its result is the most refined definition which is default to "string" accessible by all interfaces definition – even the one that doesn't have the generic angle brackets.

```
interface InterfaceGenericDefinedTwoPlace<T = string>{
  myProp:T;
}
interface InterfaceGenericDefinedTwoPlace<T>{}
interface InterfaceGenericDefinedTwoPlace{}
```

To conclude, generic must have a type defined between the < and > symbol. An empty generic is not valid since TypeScript 2.3.

3.18 ENUM

Enum is a type that enforces a limited and defined group of constant. Enum must have a name and its accepted values. Afterward, you can use the enum as a type. The consumer must use the enum with the name of the enum followed by a dot and a potential value from the defined list.

```
enum MyEnum {
  ChoiceA,
  ChoiceB,
  ChoiceC
};
const x: MyEnum = MyEnum.ChoiceA;
```

The values are all constant starting from 0 for the first item and increase by one until the end. Developers can specify a specific value by equating to an integer. There is no obligation to define every member; for example, defining the first element to 100 will set the following elements to continue the sequence by increments of one. Enum members' values can be set directly but also by using computation. There are two types of computation – a constant and one purely computed. A computed constant is a value provided from another enum or a value computed by addition, subtraction, bitwise, modulo, multiplication, division, "or," "and," "xor" operator or complement operator (~). Pure computed values come from a function.

```
enum MyEnum2 {
   ChoiceA, // 0
   ChoiceB = 100, // 100
   ChoiceC, // 101
   ChoiceD = MyEnum.ChoiceC // 2
};
```

Enum can be of string type. In that case, every member requires a value without exception.

```
enum MyStringEnum {
   ChoiceA = "A",
   ChoiceB = "B"
}
```

A mixed enum value type is acceptable if every member is defined. For example, you can have one item as an integer and another with a string type. The recommendation is not to mix types since it might be more confusing than pragmatic.

```
enum MyStringAndNumberEnum {
   ChoiceA, // 0
   ChoiceB = "B",
   ChoiceC = 100
}
```

Like interfaces, an enum can be defined in more than one place. You can start defining the enum and later define it again. In the end, all values merge into a single enum. There is one constraint with multiple definitions of a single enum, and it is that every enum must have the first element with an explicit value. If an explicit value is defined twice, only the last value will be associated with the enum when using the reverse value to an enum. Having twice the same value is not a feature of multiple definitions; a single enumeration definition can have several entries with the same value as well.

```
enum EnumA {
  ChoiceA
}
enum EnumA {
  ChoiceB = 1
}
```

Enum lets you reverse a value for integer, but not for an enum with string. It means you can use the enum name followed with the name of the constant to get the value. And, with a number, you can also use the value to get the name back. For example, an enum called Orientation with East, West, North, South could use Orientation.East to get the value zero or use Orientation[0] to get "East." The reason is that TypeScript generates a map object which gives you access using the name of the entry or the value. Here is the generated code of the orientation enum.

```
var Orientation;
(function (Orientation) {
  Orientation[Orientation["East"] = 0] = "East";
  Orientation[Orientation["West"] = 1] = "West";
  Orientation[Orientation["North"] = 2] = "North";
  Orientation[Orientation["South"] = 3] = "South";
})(Orientation || (Orientation = {}));
;
```

Enum is a good candidate to bitwise operation since the value can be explicitly set and you can use the bit shift operator. Once defined, you can use it as any variable to determine it contains one of choice or to use the ampersand (&) to check if one of choice is present. The pipe symbol (|) let you add many enum choices to a variable.

```
enum Power {
   None = 0,
   Invincibility = 1 << 0,
   Telepathy = 1 << 1,
   Invisibility = 1 << 2,
   Everything = Invincibility | Telepathy | Invisibility
}
let power: Power = Power.Invincibility | Power.Telepathy;
if (power & Power.Telepathy) {
   console.log("Power of telepathy available");
}
```

Enum can be a constant to speed up the performance. This way, during execution, instead of referencing the function generated by TypeScript to JavaScript, it will use the value. For example, without constant enum, the value set to a direction with Orientation.East will be equal to a function that looks for the value in the map to get the value. However, with a constant, the value is set in the transpiled code to "0" directly – no more function or mapping. There is not a lot of drawbacks. You can still use the enum with the dot notation and the name of one of the entry. You can also use the name of the enum with the square bracket with the name of one of the entries. However, you won't be able to use the square bracket with the value. The last difference is that constant enum doesn't allow for redefining value once initialized, which is allowed with default non-constant enum. However, in both cases, it's possible to add an entry using the square bracket. This feature is available since version 1.4 and can be turned off by using the compiler option "preserveConstEnums" and setting it to true.

```
const enum Orientation {
   East,
   West,
   North,
   South
};

let wontUseTheFunction = Orientation.East;
// Produce : var wontUseTheFunction = 0 /* East */;
```

Another feature of enum is that you can attach a function that will be accessible statically by the enum. Enum with function means that you can use Orientation.East as well as Orientation.yourFunction. Defining a function inside an enum requires the use of a namespace with an exported function.

```
enum Orientation {
  East,
  West,
  North,
  South
};
namespace Orientation {
  export function yourFunction() {
  }
}
let wontUseTheFunction = Orientation.yourFunction();
```

3.19 COMMENT

The reason comments are under the variable section even if not a variable per se is that they are mostly present to give more information about them or functions. Comment in TypeScript uses the same syntax as JavaScript. So, you can use the double slash for single line comment or use the slash stars to open a block of comments and a start slash to close the block. A case of slash star is for JSDoc style or to comment a big block of comment. You can use TypeScript to not emit any comment using the option "removeComments" of the compiler.

```
let x = 1; // This is a single line comment
/* This can be spread on
multiple
lines */
let y = 2;
```

One little detail about TypeScript is about the starting comment at the top of a file. A special syntax with the slash star followed by an exclamation mark (/*!) tells TypeScript to keep the comment. Forcing the comment is true regardless if the TypeScript's compiler option "removeComments" is true. The exclamation point is a trick to keep copyright at the top of the generated file.

3.20 MAPPED TYPE

Mapped type allows for creating a new type from an existing type. Using the term map refers to pointing existing members over a new type by a custom logic that is unique to the mapper implementation. A good example is to transform an existing interface to have all the same members but to be optional or all read-only. Mapped type brings two advantages over the previous version of Typescript that didn't support it. Before mapped type, we needed to create an additional interface to reflect the desired final state. The problem is that it is polluting the code base of several interfaces depending on how you transform the interface as well as many duplicates for each different interface that needs to be mapped. Furthermore, for each original interface, you need to synchronize all other ones every time the interface changes. It becomes rapidly hard to maintain.

```
// Before mapped type: 2 interfaces + 1 function per interface couple
interface OriginalInterface {
   x: number;
   y: string;
}

interface ReadOnlyOriginalInterface {
   readonly x: number;
   readonly y: string;
}

function mapOriginalInterfaceToBeReadOnly(
o: OriginalInterface): ReadOnlyOriginalInterface {
   return {
      x: o.x,
      y: o.y
   };
}
```

The second advantage is that without mapped type, every interface requires a function to perform the transformation. Again, this gets out of control very fast. With mapped type, you only need your transformation function and to define your mapped type. With the help of generic, the transformation function is self-sufficient to take a generic interface and returns the mapped type define which is also leveraging generic.

One well-known JavaScript function that has a mapped type already backed inside TypeScript is the "Object.freeze." The role of this function is to take a type and return the same one but everything read-only. The function has a return type of "Readonly<T>" where T is the interface to freeze. The name mapped comes from the fact that within the type there is an instruction with the keyword "in" which will loop through all the object property and prototype chain. The return type uses the lookup type which is a semantic way to indicate that the return type is not the original generic type T passed but an aggregate of all properties of this one. Here is a simplistic version of the same example as before with read-only but generic using mapped type.

```
interface OriginalInterface {
  x: number;
  y: string;
}

type ReadonlyInterface<T> = {
  readonly [P in keyof T]: T[P];
};

function genericInterfaceToReadOnly<T>(o: T): ReadonlyInterface<T> {
  return o;
}

const original: OriginalInterface = { x: 0, y: "1" };
const originalReadonly = genericInterfaceToReadOnly(original);
originalReadonly.x = 3; // error TS2540: Cannot assign to 'x'
                        //because it is a constant or a read-only property.
```

TypeScript has a few mapped types that you can explore by looking in lib.d.t.s. The "Partial" mapped type sets every property optional. "Pick" allows taking a subset of an interface. Here is an example with "freeze" that set every property "Readonly".

```
const originalReadonlyFromTS = Object.freeze(original);
originalReadonlyFromTS.x = 3; // error TS2540: Cannot assign to 'x' because it is a constant or a read-only property.
```

Map type can add a modifier (like read-only or optional) and since version 2.8 can also remove modifiers.

```
type RemoveReadonlyAndOptional<T> = {
  -readonly [P in keyof T]-?: T[P]
}
```

The example shows that by using the minus sign it's possible to remove read-only or the optional.

CHAPTER 4: OBJECT

TypeScript has many object types. In this section, we will see the difference between the two objects which are confusingly called Object and object, one that starts with an uppercase "O" and the other one with a lowercase "o." We will also see how the curly bracket brings a third object type. The lowercase object comes not only from "Object.create" but also if you instantiate a class in TypeScript. It represents all types that are not primitive, which means not Boolean, number, string, symbol, null and undefined.

4.1 CURLY BRACES

TypeScript can create an object using the curly braces – it is an object literal like in JavaScript. The limitation is that you must define every member right at the initialization time. The advantage is that it's a quick way to organize data. It's also a natural way to organize data coming from a JSON Payload. For example, executing a request to receive a payload will provide you an object that is a literal one. TypeScript is a structural language, and hence doesn't need to have a name. This works great for cases of response where you do not need to map all the data to a type. With a structural type, you can cast the data and have the structure mapped for you without having to instantiate anything.

When not working with data coming from a third party or across the wire, you can use a variable and specify the type using a colon and then use the curly braces to set the value. TypeScript will catch at compilation type that something is missing if the type changes.

```
let x: { x: number, y: string } = { x: 1, y: "2" };
// Below code is similar, but reusable with a type (as interface)
interface MyTypeWithTwoMembers { x: number, y: string }
let x2: MyTypeWithTwoMembers = { x: 1, y: "2" };
```

On the contrary, this is not the case if the type is not defined since it will rely on the new structure and might continue to fit in subsequent code.

An important detail is that instead of defining a variable with a type, with the colon, and just relying on the equality to set values and then use a cast to force the type, it will set the variable values even if not complete and will allow you to use the variable with the type. Casting is dangerous since you might end up having a typed variable that is not fully structured, thus having a runtime error. The following example is built on the previous one. The example shows a member called "x" of type number. The value is set to "1" and if we do not cast would be of an anonymous type that accepts only the "x" member of type "number." However, since we cast to an interface, the actual type of the variable is the interface one. However, the member "y" is missing which would result in an unexpected result at execution time since "y" was not defined to be of type string or undefined but only string.

```
let myObjectTypedWithCurlyType3 = { x: 1 } as MyTypeWithTwoMembers;
```

It's important to note that casting curly braces to "any" should not be considered a viable strategy since it opens the door to set members to an unexpected value which becomes an issue like every "any" type by losing the rigidity of type. Casting to an interface or type should be moderate in your code. Some valid use case is when receiving a payload from an Ajax call which will always come in "any" type. Casting is allowed since the API should return the response in a format that is well known and match your TypeScript-defined interfaces/types. This approach doesn't guarantee validation if the Ajax's response contract changes. In the case of a change, the code will still compile and will fail at runtime when the expected value is undefined. Casting will be discussed later in this book.

On a final note, objects created with curly bracket have access to all members of the Object type (capital O). Further details are described shortly.

4.2 NEW

TypeScript can create an object by instantiating a class using the keyword "new." The chapter around object-oriented will cover all the benefits. In a nutshell, TypeScript lets you use the full set of object-oriented features even if targeting ECMAScript before 2015 which is not available with Object or literal object. It means that if you want to use polymorphism, have multiple instances of a type, use decorator, be able to use a pattern like dependency of injection or even just being able to mock specific functions of an object; the use of the class is mandatory. Creating an object with "new" creates an instance of an object which inherits all characteristics of the uppercase Object.

4.3 LOWERCASE OBJECT

With TypeScript 2.2, the lowercase object type was born. The type englobes all types that are not primitive. It's easy to get confused with uppercase Object which is common to every kind of object. Here is the list of the types that are not an object: undefined, null, number, string, Boolean, and symbol.

4.4 UPPERCASE OBJECT

The uppercase Object is the one from JavaScript which gives basic functions like "toString," "hasOwnProperty," etc. These functions are also available naturally by the prototype chain if you are using curly braces to create an empty object. Direct use of the "Object" is rare. However, when you instantiate a class, it summons a new uppercase Object.

Deciding between the lowercase object and uppercase Object can be confusing. The rule of thumb is to use the lowercase object when a non-primitive is required. The use of the uppercase Object is to access one of the members from the ECMAScript Object, like "hasOwnProperty," "toString," etc.

4.5 INDEX SIGNATURE

JavaScript allows accessing object's member by using the squared brackets and the name of the member between them. It allows for reaching a value dynamically without having to use the dot notation. This technic is called accessing by index signature, and it is available to any object for assignation or reading value.

TypeScript brings the game a notch higher with better support for improved control over the manipulation of the index. First, you can only access via string or number. With JavaScript, you could use an object which would fall back to the "toString" function, for example, which leads to some issues when using with an object because of "toString" returns "[object Object]."

```
let objectIndex: { x: number, y: string } = { x: 1, y: "2" };
objectIndex["x"] = 2;
objectIndex[0] = 1;
// objectIndex[{ x: 1 }] = 123; // Doesn't compile
console.log(objectIndex); // { '0': 1, x: 2, y: '2' }
```

TypeScript with the option "noImplicitAny" to true won't allow accessing a member not defined when working on a strongly typed. This option should be set to true for every new project because it enforces a stronger type validation.

```
let objectIndex: { x: number, y: string } = { x: 1, y: "2" };
objectIndex["x"] = 2;
objectIndex[0] = 1;        // Doesn't compile
objectIndex["asd"] = 1; // Doesn't compile
```

Index signature can define members with an identifier with square brackets. The identifier type can only be a string or a number. Index signature can be useful if you want to control the type of key to a dynamic assignation as well as the type to be returned. For example, imagine having a custom map type that allows for having a string key and return a specific type of object. Having a defined index signature allows for having a strongly typed key (string or number) that can hold an explicit type.

```
interface MyStringDictionary {
  [key: number]: string;
}
const dict1: MyStringDictionary = {
  [100]: "hundred",
  [200]: "two hundreds"
};
// Or more generic (with string key variation)
interface MyGenericDictionary<T> {
  [id: string]: T;
}
const dict2: MyGenericDictionary<string> = {
  ["100"]: "hundred",
  ["200"]: "two hundreds"
};
```

The interface defined with members and an index type that use a string as the key must have all its members to be of string type.

```
interface MyStringDictionaryWithMembers {
  [key: string]: string;
  m1: string;
  m2: number; // Won't compile, must be a string
}
```

A way to work around this restriction would be to have the index to be a union of many types which would allow all union types to be available as member type.

```
interface MyStringDictionaryWithMembers2 {
  [key: string]: string | number;
  m1: string;
  m2: number;
}
```

In the case of an index map with a number, members can be of any type.

```
interface MyStringDictionaryWithMembers3 {
   [key: number]: string;
   m1: string;
   m2: number;
   m3: boolean;
   m4: { x: string, y: number }
}
```

It makes possible to define two indexes: one with a string key, one with a number key. However, beware that you'll have to change the return type of the string key to return not only the type you want the map but also all the type of members of the object. TypeScript is stricter with index type of string by design.

```
interface MyStringDictionaryWithTwoMap {
   [key: number]: string;
   [key: string]: string;
   // [key: string]: number; // Doesn't compile
}
```

Version 2.7 brings the possibility of accessing property using constant and symbol. This is a minor improvement because before 2.7, it was possible to access (read and write) with a constant or symbol but not defining a field in an interface or type.

```
const Foo = "Foo";
const Bar = "Bar";
const Zaz = "Zaz";

const objectWithConstantProperties = {
   [Foo]: 100,
   [Bar]: "hello",
   [Zaz]: () => { },
};

let a12 = x[Foo];
let b2334 = x[Bar];
```

The syntax is the same as when accessing the field for consumption. It uses the square brackets with the constant or the symbol.

```
// const SERIALIZE = Symbol("serialize-method-key"); //or const
const SERIALIZE = "serialize-method-key";
interface Serializable {
  [SERIALIZE](obj: {}): string;
}
```

CHAPTER 5: VARIABLE ADVANCED

In this chapter, we will cover more advanced variable feature that TypeScript supports.

5.1 INTERSECT

TypeScript can manipulate types by combining any of them. The first way is to specify a type to be an intersection type. You can use the ampersand to intersect many types. In the end, the type will have the sum of all members.

```
type T1 = { x: string };
type T2 = { y: number };
type T3 = { z: boolean };
type IntersectType1 = T1 & T2 & T3;
type IntersectType2 = T1 & T2;
type IntersectType3 = T3 & T1;
const inter1: T1 = { x: "x1", y: 2 }; // Won't compile
const inter2: T1 & T2 = { x: "x1", y: 2 }; // Compile
const inter3: IntersectType2 = { x: "x1", y: 2 }; // Compile
```

Interfaces work well with intersecting as well.

```
interface I1 {
  x: string;
}
interface I2 {
  y: number;
}
interface I3 {
  z: boolean;
}
type IntersectWithInterface = I1 & I2 & I3;
const with3Interfaces: IntersectWithInterface = { x: "1", y: 1, z: true };
```

Or it can be used for extending other interfaces. However, intersect shines with a dynamic composition of types while with the inheritance of interfaces would require creating additional interfaces to inherit existing interface and eventually would pollute the code base depending on what must be combining.

```
interface CombineI1 extends I1, I2, I3 {}
interface CombineI2 extends I1, I2 {}
interface CombineI3 extends I3, I1 {}
```

Setting the result of intersecting into a variable is more reusable and pragmatic than inheritance. However, it is also convenient to use an intersect on-the-fly for a parameter or a return type.

```
function intersectOnTheFly(t: I1 & I2){ }
```

Intersect and generic type can be combined to give flexibility. In the following example, the function is generic and combines the two generic types in the return type.

```
function intersectGeneric<TT1, TT2>(t1: TT1, t2: TT2): TT1 & TT2 {
  const returnValue = <TT1 & TT2>{};
  for (let index in t1) {
    (returnValue as TT1)[index] = t1[index];
  }
  for (let index in t2) {
    (returnValue as TT2)[index] = t2[index];
  }
  return returnValue;
}
```

5.2 LITERAL TYPE

A literal type sets a single value to a variable's type. Initially, TypeScript supported only a string. Nowadays, a literal type can be a Boolean, a number or an enum.

```
let x : "test";
let y : 123;
let z : true;
```

The concept of having a value that controls the data type flow can be extended beyond type checking to narrow down to a single type within a union. A return type can borrow the concept of narrowing by depending on the value's discriminant field. The result is to have a specific return type. Imagine the scenario where a method can return a cat or a dog. The function will return a cat interface if the discriminant is a "cat." Otherwise, the function returns a "dog" interface. A discriminant is powerful since the consumer can compare the return value and narrow its value to a single type automatically. Another example could be a response from an Ajax call which returns a success or a failure. In the case of a failure, the returned interface can have HTTP status and error and when a success the payload. Instead of having a single type that contains all these fields, you can return a type that unites a successful request and a failed request. The consumer can then check the discriminant and leverage the automatic narrowed type to fulfill both scenarios with a rich experience that contains only the field required depending on the response.

```
interface Success {
  success: true;
  httpCode: string;
  payload: string;
}
interface Failure {
  success: false;
  errorMessage: string;
}

function ajax(url: string): Success | Failure {
  return { success: false, errorMessage: "Error!" }; // Hardcoded failure
}
function ajaxCall(): string {
  const ajaxResult = ajax("http://blablac.com");
  if (ajaxResult.success === true) {
    return ajaxResult.payload; // Access to all Success interface members
  } else {
    return ajaxResult.errorMessage; // Access to all Failure interface
members
  }
}
const result = ajaxCall();
```

A literal type declared as a constant without specifying a type are automatically set to the type of the string associated with them. An implicit declaration of literal type sets the type to the type of the value.

However, setting a string to a “let” variable instead of “const” doesn’t set the type to the string value, but to the type of string. The explicit value is the only valid path with “let” to set a literal type. Another interesting characteristic is that if you create a “let” variable and you associate a constant literal type, the “let” variable will be a string and not the literal. It opens the definition to a broader scope since the let allows to redefine the value at any time. Here are examples that illustrate the difference between “const” and “let” with literal type.

```
const literalType1 = "c";          // Type is not string, but "c"
const literalType2: "c" = "c"; // Same as above
let literalType3 = "c";            // Type is string
let literalType4: "c" = "c";     // Type is not string, but "c"
```

5.3 UNION

A union type is more common because it’s often used to indicate that a variable can be one type or another. For example, a member could be a string or undefined. Union types are the strongly typed way to allow multiples type for a function too. If you have a function that can take a string or an object and depend on the type acting different, the union can do the job. “Any” type would also work, but the problem is that “any” allows being everything while in reality, you want to have only a limited type of parameter. With “any” it would also be at runtime that you could catch if something is not assigned correctly, but with the union, it’s at compilation time. The return type of a function can be a union. A function may return a specific object or undefined, for example, or return a number or a string.

```
let u1: string | boolean = true;
type UStringBoolean = string | boolean;
let u2: UStringBoolean = true;
```

Since TypeScript 2.0, the concept of tagged union type has risen. Imagine that you created a new type with the union of several interfaces. At some point in the execution of your system, there might be a need to narrow the type. This need may arise simply by wanting to do a specific action that requires knowing the type with accuracy. The possibility of being from many types complexify the use of a union type. Using a particular feature of a specific type needs to give TypeScript a hint. Otherwise, only shared features are available.

TypeScript has many ways to determine which type within the union is the value. You can always check for specific members that are unique to each interface and use a method to tell TypeScript which interface it is. We will see that technic in the "type checking" section of this book. However, this requires creating a single method per interface. To avoid convoluted code, the use of tagged union type becomes handy. The concept is simple. Every interface needs a common field with the same name, but a different type. The type can be anything unique. A common use is to specify to this discriminant field a type of a unique string. It is to be noted that the field type is not a string, which would allow all kinds of string, but a specific one which means that only this string. The discriminant is built with something called a string literal type, as we will describe in this book. Up to now, nothing is really specific to TypeScript. However, where TypeScript shines is when you compare the discriminant field to the type specified in one of the interfaces, that TypeScript will automatically narrow down the type to the proper related interface. For example, you can create a switch statement directly on the attribute using the discriminant field used for this purpose which is shared across all union types, hence available without any casting and creates a case for each interface using their unique string.

```
interface InterfaceA {
  discriminant: "InterfaceA"; // This is not a string type, but InterfaceA type
  m0: number;
}
interface InterfaceB {
  discriminant: "InterfaceB"; // This is not a string type, but InterfaceB type
  m1: string;
}
interface InterfaceC {
  discriminant: "InterfaceC"; // This is not a string type, but InterfaceC type
  m2: string;
}
function unionWithDiscriminant(p: InterfaceA | InterfaceB | InterfaceC) {
  switch (p.discriminant) { // Only common members available
    case "InterfaceA":
      console.log(p.m0); // Only InterfaceA members available
      break;
    case "InterfaceB":
      console.log(p.m1); // Only InterfaceB members available
      break;
    case "InterfaceC":
      console.log(p.m2); // Only InterfaceC members available
      break;
  }
}
```

TypeScript version 2.7 brings a change with classes and union. From 2.7, union keeps the type of classes in a union the same structure. Before 2.7, the type was narrowed.

5.4 TYPE CHECKING

Some variables can be of multiple known types which open the door to desire to narrow down to which type is the variable. TypeScript can achieve this by using mostly JavaScript check at runtime but also can infer the type at design time and allow a compilation validation, as well as an Intellisense, once checked.

5.4.1 TYPEOF

JavaScript has "typeof" which is also available in TypeScript. However, TypeScript is powerful enough to scope down the multiple types variable to the type check on this one return true. Functions with a parameter that supports a number and a string with the use of a union can use "typeof." When using "typeof" in a condition, if the result is positive, the type will be scoped down to the tested type. Without using "typeof", the variable would be usable only with members that are shared by both types. The reason is that TypeScript wouldn't be able to figure out the actual type. "typeof" is limited to number, string, Boolean and symbol. For determining the type of an object with the constructor, you must use "instanceof."

```
let variable: string | boolean | number = 1;
function displayVariable(param: string | boolean | number) {
  if (typeof param === "string") {
    console.log(param.length); // Narrowed down to string
  }
  if (typeof param === "boolean") {
    console.log(param ? "Yes" : "No"); // Narrowed down to boolean
  }
  if (typeof param === "number") {
    console.log(param.toPrecision(2)); // Narrowed down to number
  }
}
displayVariable(variable); // Display 1.0
```

5.4.2 INSTANCEOF

"Instanceof" also comes from JavaScript and executes at runtime. Nevertheless, TypeScript can handle the test operator that is looking at the prototype chain to figure out the type of object. Like "typeof," if the comparison with "instanceof" is positive, the type is narrowed down to the checked type. "Instanceof" cannot be used for Interface checks and is limited to a class comparison since it relies on the constructor function.

```
class C1 {}
class C2 {}
const c1 = new C1();
if (c1 instanceof C1) {
   console.log("c1 is an instance of C1");
}
if (c1 instanceof C2) {
   console.log("c1 is an instance of C1");
}
```

There is one particularity since TypeScript 2.1 in regard to inheritance and "instanceOf". In cases where C2 extends C1, C2 returns true to the check on C1 and C2. However, if any of the prototype chains extends Error, Array or Map, then each constructor must call the "setPrototypeOf" in each constructor.

```
class C100 extends Error {
  constructor() {
    super();
    Object.setPrototypeOf(this, C100.prototype);
  }
}
class C200 extends C100 {
  constructor() {
    super();
    Object.setPrototypeOf(this, C200.prototype);
  }
}
const c100 = new C200();
if (c100 instanceof C100) {
  console.log("c100 is an instance of C100");
}
if (c100 instanceof C200) {
  console.log("c100 is an instance of C200");
}
if (c100 instanceof Error) {
  console.log("c100 is an instance of Error");
}
```

Before version 2.7, "instanceOf" operator was relying on the structure of the object. With version 2.7, the operator uses the inheritance chain. The following example shows the difference. The "ChildB" and "ChildC" have the same structure. With versions prior to 2.7, "instanceOf" compares by the structure and hence the first conditional statement accepts "ChildB" and "ChildD." The "else" condition is never reachable because the two conditions before this one cover all cases. With version 2.7, the first conditional block only lets "ChildB," the second block "ChildC" and all others "ChildD."

```
class BaseClassA { }
class ChildB extends BaseClassA { }
class ChildC extends BaseClassA { }
class ChildD extends BaseClassA { c: string = "c value" }

function compareWithInstanceOf(x: ChildB | ChildC | ChildD) {
  if (x instanceof ChildB) {
    console.log("Found an instance of B");
    x; // B (V2.6: B | D)
  }
  else if (x instanceof ChildC) {
    console.log("Found an instance of C");
    x; // C
  }
  else {
    console.log("Found an instance not known");
    x; // D (V2.6 never)
  }
}

compareWithInstanceOf(new ChildB);
compareWithInstanceOf(new ChildC);
compareWithInstanceOf(new ChildD);
```

The "instanceOf" checks that the left part derives from the right part.

5.4.3 UNDEFINED

Checking for undefined is something done regularly since many parameters are often optional, hence undefined when not provided. The triple equals perform the comparison against the undefined keyword. The same is true for checking for null. You can use a condition with or without using double or triple equals to check null. However, avoiding using the equal sign can lead to issues if you are checking a Boolean or number variable. The reason is that it will not only check for null or undefined but also for the value "true". The coercion of the three values is not a desired situation but if you are looking for an object which you know will never change to a Boolean type or number, then you are fine. However, things change, so the safest practice is to be explicit and check for what you are checking. If you need to check for null and for undefined, you can always use the double equals to null or undefined which will do the job, or again, be explicit for both.

```
function checkIfDefined<T>(value?: T): void {
// Better approach would be : (value !== null && value !== undefined)
  if (value) {
    console.log("Value " + value + " is defined");
  } else {
    console.log("Value " + value + " is NOT defined");
  }
}

checkIfDefined(null); // Not defined (okay!)
checkIfDefined(undefined); // Not defined (okay!)
checkIfDefined(true); // Defined (okay!)
checkIfDefined(false); // Not defined (!!! Unexpected !!!)
checkIfDefined(0); // Not defined (!!! Unexpected !!!)
checkIfDefined(1);  // Defined (okay!)
```

5.4.4 INTERFACE

Type checking is trickier when determining an interface type. The reason is that interfaces are a TypeScript concept and doesn't translate to JavaScript. In other words, Typescript erases types and hence looking for the runtime is impossible. With the actual version of Typescript, there are two technics to check the type of an interface.

The first technic creates a function as a custom user-defined type guard. You need to create a single function for each of your interface in the global scope or anywhere you want other than in the interface since we need to define the code. The function must have at least a single parameter of type "any" which allows every object to be passed on. The return type is special. It consists of the evaluated variable name followed by the keyword "is" and the evaluated interface against which we compare. The peculiar declaration indicates to TypeScript which type to narrow down when the function returns true. The idea is to evaluate if some members are in the object to determine the actual type. This work at runtime since TypeScript is structural and you are looking to see if a piece of the structure is defined.

However, this is not very flexible when interfaces change a lot, or if you have a lot of interfaces or if interfaces contain a lot of members.

```
interface ICheck1 extends ICheck2 {
  m1: number;
}
interface ICheck2 {
  m2: string;
}
function checkInterfaceICheck1(obj: any): obj is ICheck1 {
  return (obj as ICheck1).m1 !== undefined;
}
function checkInterfaceICheck2(obj: any): obj is ICheck2 {
  return (obj as ICheck2).m2 !== undefined;
}
function print(obj: ICheck1 | ICheck2): void {
  if (checkInterfaceICheck1(obj)) {
    console.log("I have access to m1", obj.m1);
  }
  if (checkInterfaceICheck2(obj)) {
    console.log("I have access to m2", obj.m2);
  }
}
const obj1: ICheck1 = { m1: 1, m2: "2" };
const obj2: ICheck2 = { m2: "2" };
console.log("Object1");
print(obj1);
console.log("Object2");
print(obj2);
/*
Object1
I have access to m1 1
I have access to m2 2
Object2
I have access to m2 2
*/
```

A second way that litigates in part some of the burdens of writing to much code is to add a discriminator that is of the type of a unique string. The detail here is to not have a discriminator of string type but of a string. It means that you have to use a member of the discriminator with a colon to a string. This one cannot change by its nature of being of the type of the string inserted. Each of your interfaces must have a unique discriminator. A wise choice is to use the name of the interface. Once that is set, you can create a function that lookup for the discriminator instead of a set of members. The function you create needs to be with a return type of the object expected. Again, this way still as a lot of boilerplate since you must define one function per interface. However, you can by-pass the function as well by just comparing the discriminator; this is called literal type guard, and TypeScript is smart enough to narrow the type as well. Another difference is the discriminant; it's a single one per interface hence won't work similarly as the member check which could find out inheritance since members are available down the chain of inheritance.

```
interface ICheck_Base{
  basem1:string;
}
interface ICheck1_2 extends ICheck_Base {
  kind: "ICheck1_2";
  m1: number;
}
interface ICheck2_2 extends ICheck_Base {
  kind: "ICheck2_2";
  m2: string;
}
function print(obj: ICheck1_2 | ICheck2_2): void {
  if (obj.kind === "ICheck1_2") {
    console.log("I have access to m1", obj.m1);
  }
  if (obj.kind === "ICheck2_2") {
    console.log("I have access to m2", obj.m2);
  }
}
const obj1_1: ICheck1_2 = { kind: "ICheck1_2", m1: 1, basem1: "2" };
const obj2_2: ICheck2_2= { kind: "ICheck2_2", m2: "2", basem1: "123" };
console.log("Object1");
print(obj1_1);
console.log("Object2");
print(obj2_2);
/*
Object1
I have access to m1 1
Object2
I have access to m2 2
*/
```

Similarly, you can use a switch case on the type instead of the if statement. The switch operator has a default case, which acts as an "else." In both cases, this fallthrough branching is a great way to catch undefined type. To do so, you need to define a default case where you set a return variable of type "never" which you assign the variable you are testing. In the case, you add a new interface with a new discriminator, and it will fail to compile since the new interface would fall into the default which is wrong since the type is never, which is not the case. TypeScript requires the compiler option "strictNullCheck" to be turned on to use leverage this pattern. The technic with the discriminator is called "discriminated union."

```
interface ICheckBase_3 {
  baseField:string;
}
interface ICheck1_3 extends ICheckBase_3 {
  kind: "ICheck1_3";
  m1: number;
}
interface ICheck2_3 {
  kind: "ICheck2_3";
  m2: string;
}
function print(obj: ICheck1_3 | ICheck2_3): void {
  switch (obj.kind) {
    case "ICheck1_3":
      console.log("I have access to m1", obj.m1);
      break;
    case "ICheck2_3":
      console.log("I have access to m2", obj.m2);
      break;
    default:
      unhandledChoiceFromEnum(obj);
  }
}
function unhandledChoiceFromEnum(x: never): never {
  throw new Error("Choice not defined");
}
```

The discriminator technique only works when the base interface doesn't have a discriminator. The reason is that it is not possible to define the same field in the inheritance chain more than once.

5.5 TUPLE

A tuple type is an array of defined elements. To declare a tuple, you use the square brackets, but instead of specifying a value, you use a type. A tuple can handle many different types. The tuple uses the same syntax for other types. The declaration of a variable and the assignation have no difference. TypeScript checks for type during assignation.

```
let myTuple: [number, string];
myTuple = [1, "test"];
const numberVariable: number = myTuple[0];
const stringVariable: string = myTuple[1];
```

Tuples are converted to a simple array when transpiled to JavaScript. It means that TypeScript lets you assign to tuple beyond the number of the type defined in the squared brackets if the variable defined beyond the range is either of the type defined in the tuple. For example, if you define a tuple to be a number and string, you can define a third variable to string or number but not Boolean or any object.

```
myTuple[3] = "one more";
myTuple[4] = 2;
myTuple[5] = true; // Won't compile (number|string only)
```

With version 2.7, TypeScript has fixed length property. The notion of length ensures that tuples have the same length and same type at their corresponding positions to be assignable.

```
let firstTuple: [number, number] = [1, 2];
let secondTuple: [number, number, number] = [3, 4, 5];
secondTuple = firstTuple; // Doesn't compile type mismatch
firstTuple = secondTuple; // Doesn't compile length incompatible
```

5.6 ALIAS

An alias or type alias allows for creating a new type from existing types. Furthermore, it is a way to enhance an existing type by combining different types. An alias doesn't have a special keyword and uses the keyword "type" to generate a new type from existing ones. Type can create a new type of copied members from several types.

5.6.1 TYPE

To create an alias with type, it requires using an existing type separated by the pipe symbol (union) or the ampersand (intersect). It's also possible to use "typeof" to extract the type of a variable.

```
type Alias1 = number | string;
const al1: Alias1 = 1;
const al2: Alias1 = "1";

type Alias2 = Alias1 | boolean;
const al3: Alias2 = 2;
const al4: Alias2 = "2";
const al5: Alias2 = false;

interface IA1 { m: string };
interface IA2 { n: number };
type Alias3 = IA1 & IA2;
const al6: Alias3 = { m: "3", n: 3 };
```

5.6.2 GENERIC TYPE ALIAS

Type aliases can be generic and can be a reference to themselves. For example, you can create a generic type that has a member that is a generic list. You can also create a type that has a member of the same type creating an infinite chain.

```
type GenericAlias1<T> = {
  id: T;
  linkedList?: GenericAlias1<T>
};
const ga1: GenericAlias1<number> = {
  id: 1,
  linkedList: {
    id: 2
  }
}
```

5.6.3 STRUCTURAL BEHAVIOR

Type aliases work under the same core TypeScript principle that the language is structural and not nominal. So, if you are creating a type from a string, you could assign a string directly without passing through the type. While this example may look simple, you can push the boundary by having a complex type and be able to pass an interface that has the same members.

```
type TypeS0 = string;
const ts0: string = "String";
const ts1: TypeS0 = "String as well";

type TypeS1 = { id: string };
interface IS1 { id: string };
let ts2: TypeS1;
const ts3: IS1 = { id: "123" };
ts2 = ts3;
```

To make a type more "nominal," you'll need to make its structure unique. This technic works also for an interface. The trick is to add a member with a unique name and value. For example, you can use a property named "kind" and the value "type1". If we return to our minimalist example of a string, now the type requires having the string as well as a member named "kind" of type "type1". This technic is called "brand" member.

```
type TypeS2 = { id: string, kind: "types2" };
interface IS2 { id: string, kind: "is2" };
let ts4: TypeS2;
const ts5: IS2 = { id: "123", kind: "is2" };
ts4 = ts5; // Doesn't work! kind should be "types2"
```

5.6.4 ALIAS WITH INTERFACE

It's also possible to use interface to alias. An interface can inherit another interface and use the hierarchy as an alias technic. However, alias built with type reduces the redundancy that induces interface in favor of composition. Alias with interface doesn't allow to build from primitive directly because of the inheritance model. Neither interface allows being defined with the union symbol. The extension with "extends" only intersects additional type. A workaround to have the union functionality would be to extend interface with optional members. However, this creates overhead when an interface may be used in a union or intersect by duplicating the interface to have both optional and not optional members.

```
interface IA10 { m: string };
interface IA20 { n: number };
interface AliasWithInterface extends IA10, IA20 { }
const useAlias: AliasWithInterface = { m: "m1", n: 1 };
```

5.6.5 BRANDED ALIAS

An alias that is also similar can be branded during initialization with an intersection (using the ampersand sign) and add a property with a type of a specific value desired for the type. A common example is when having a type alias for currency.

```
type USD = number & { name: "USD" };
type CAD = number & { name: "CAD" };
const usd:USD = 1 as USD;
const cad:CAD = 2 as CAD;

function sum(c1: USD, c2: USD): number {
   return (c1 + c2);
}
sum(usd, usd);
sum(cad, usd); // Error!
```

An interface can benefit from branding by creating a private member that will turn the interface structurally unique. TypeScript's interface name doesn't matter in differentiating types. However, TypeScript differentiates an interface with a unique field. It can be a unique field name across interfaces or the same field name with unique type regardless of the usage of the field (used or not). The importance is to have a unique structure for each interface. However, since an interface cannot have a private field, you need to use the old trick of prefixing with an underscore which is a hack. Using an underscore with a unique field is a technic used by the TypeScript team. The prefix trick should be used with moderation to avoid confusion between what can or cannot be used in your code. This addition to the code is available to all consumers but in reality with a very narrow role of differentiator. The issue lies in the cast which can cause an issue by coercing an object that might not have all members defined or to assign any value to the branded variable. We will see more about this drawback in the casting section.

```
interface BaseIpo { m: string };
interface Ipo1 extends BaseIpo { _kindIpo1: any; }
interface Ipo2 extends BaseIpo { _kindIpo2: any; }
type Ipo3 = { _kindIpo3: any; } & BaseIpo;

let ipo1: Ipo1 = { m: "1" } as Ipo1;
let ipo2: Ipo2 = { m: "1" } as Ipo2
let ipo3: Ipo3 = { m: "1" } as Ipo3;
let ipo3_without_cast: Ipo3 = { m: "1", _kindIpo3:"" }; // No cast
ipo1 = ipo2; // Doesn't work since the underscore field is different
```

Branding with the type "any" is not particularly appealing. This is why instead of using a different name with the same type, it's more favorable to use the type checking with a discriminant technic (see the previous section). It means to have the same name field but with a unique type. However, type checking might fall short if you need inheritance support which doesn't work for a unique field.

5.7 CAST

TypeScript casts use two different forms: <> or "as." The former enters into conflict with the JSX/TSX format which is now getting popular because of React, hence not recommended. The latter is as good, and it works in all situations.

The first way is to use the symbols < and > with the type desired in-between. The syntax requires the cast before the variable that we want to coerce.

The second way is to use the keyword "as." "as" is placed after the variable we want to cast followed by the type to cast.

```
const cast1: number = <number>1;
const cast2: number = 1 as number;
```

Casting is a delicate subject since you can cast every variable into something without completely respecting the contract into which we cast. For example, you can have an interface that requires many fields and cast an empty object to that interface, and it will compile even if you do not have the members. The fallacy of the cast when the underlying object doesn't respect the type schema is one reason why it's better if you can assign a type to the variable and not cast. However, there is a situation where you must cast. For example, if you receive a JSON payload from an Ajax call, this one will be by nature "any" since the response of an Ajax is undetermined until the consumer does the call. In that case, you must cast to manipulate the data in a typed fashion in the rest of your application. The constraint here is that you must be sure that you are receiving the data in a format that provide all expected members. Otherwise, it would be wiser to define these members to be optional (undefined as well as the expected type).

```
interface ICast1 { m1: string }
interface ICast2 { m1: string, m2: string }

let icast1: ICast1 = { m1: "m1" };
let icast2: ICast2 = { m1: "m1", m2: "m2" };
let icast3: ICast1 = icast2; // work without cast because of the structure
icast2 = icast1; // doesn't work, miss a member
let icast4: ICast2 = icast1 as ICast2; // work but m2 undefined
console.log(icast4); // { m1: 'm1' } // m2 is missing even if not optional
```

Casting has some restrictions. For instance, you cannot cast a typed object into something that is not a subtype. If you have TypeC that inherits TypeB that inherits TypeA, you can cast a TypeC to TypeA or TypeB without problem or TypeB to TypeA without casting. However, going the other way around requires a cast. Nevertheless, there are issues in both cases. When going from a subtype to a type, without casting, the problem is that TypeScript will validate that you can only access the public type from the desired interface. However, under the hood, the object still contains all the members. For example (see below), TypeB has two members; when casting, it only exposes at design time the first member which is in TypeA. However, printing the object reveals both members are still there. The lack of cohesion between the type's schema and the actual object structure is an important detail. For example, sending an object to an API without manually grooming the object may pass more information than anticipated.

The second issue is with casting. Since casting coerces by saying to TypeScript that you know what you are doing, it won't complain. However, non-optional members not present will be undefined even if the contract specifies that the type must have the member. You can see an example below when an object of TypeA (base interface) is cast down to TypeB. The cast coerces the change of type, but "m2" is still not present. While it is good enough for TypeScript that you manually override the validation, it can be problematic if later in the code you try to access "m2" and believe that this one cannot be undefined. In fact, this can cause a runtime error if you try to access a function of the member.

```
interface ITypeA { m1: string }
interface ITypeB extends ITypeA { m2: string }
interface ITypeC extends ITypeB { m3: string }
const typea: ITypeA = { m1: "m1" };
const typeb: ITypeB = { m1: "m1", m2: "m2" };
let typeb2: ITypeB = typea as ITypeB; // Work (m2 will be missing!!!)
let typea2: ITypeA = typeb; // No cast needed
console.log(typea2); // { m1: 'm1', m2: 'm2' } However, only m1 is accessible
at compilation
```

However, casting to a string won't work. However, casting to any and then casting to string will work. Again, the sliding ground is with any.

```
let aNumberToCast: number = 1;
// let aString: string = aNumberToCast as string; // Doesn't work
let aString: string = aNumberToCast as any as string;
```

The best practice with casting is to try to cast as little as possible. To cast at a strategic area of your code like when getting untyped object is a smart and limited place. When you need to create a new type, it's better to assign a type (explicit declaration) than casting. Doing so, provide IntelliSense support and the compiler protection which keep the code stable with the expected type.

5.8 KEYOF

"keyof" is a subtype of String that allows extracting members name from a type or interface. The main goal of "keyof" is to define a set of valid members' name. For example, you may have a public function that takes the direction as a string for convenience. Defining this parameter as a string would be an open the door to accept anything. However, using the keyword "keyof" followed by the type that contains a union of the four cardinal points would limit the allowed string to the four values.

```
// Interface's members
interface InterfaceWithMembers {
   id: number; title: string; createdBy: Date;
}

const members: keyof InterfaceWithMembers = "id"; // Only accept id, title or createdBy

// Type's values
type TypeToKeyOf = "north" | "south" | "east" | "west";
function fKeyOfParameter(direction: TypeToKeyOf) { }
fKeyOfParameter("no"); // Doesn't compile
fKeyOfParameter("north");
```

Generic can use "keyof." For example, you can have a function that takes the first parameter of type "T" and the second parameter of type R extends "keyof" T. The extend "keyof" of the second parameter means that the second parameter scopes down the potential value of the first argument. It is dynamic, and TypeScript provides full validation at design type and transpilation time. In the following example, the interface contains three members that are the only possible string value to pass as the second parameter. The return type is the type of the member K of the object T which are both passed by parameter.

```
const iWithMembersForKeyOf: InterfaceWithMembers =
   { id: 1, title: "1", createdBy: new Date() };

function prop<T, K extends keyof T>(obj: T, key: K): T[K] {
   return obj[key];
}
const id = prop(iWithMembersForKeyOf, "id"); //the value 1 of type number
```

5.9 EXCEPTION

TypeScript follows ECMAScript in terms of exception. You can fire a new exception by using the keyword "throw" followed by an instance of the exception you desire. It's always better to throw an object and not a string directly. Throwing an object comes with the whole execution stack since the object must inherit from the base interface "Error." This interface defines a name, a message, and the stack. The only case where you do not need to throw an instance of an exception is when using the ErrorConstructor which lets you throw the error directly by using "throw Error("Message here that is optional").

```
function throw1() {
  throw "error in string";
}

function throw2() {
  throw Error("Message Here");
}

function throw3() {
  const err: Error = {
    name: "Error",
    message: "Message"
  };
  throw err;
}
```

The "try" and "catch" structure handles exception like many well-known languages like Java and C#. The "try" englobes the code that is susceptible to throw an exception. The code executed in error will send the exception to the "catch" only if an exception occurs. The catch statement has a single parameter. The parameter is the exception object. It's possible to provide a "finally" block after the "catch" that is executed every time after the execution regardless of having an exception or not.

```
try {
    throw1();
} catch (e) {
    console.log("Exception 1", e); // String
}
try {
    throw2();
} catch (e) {
    console.log("Exception 2", e); // Full stack
}
try {
    throw3();
} catch (e) {
    console.log("Exception 2", e); // Object
}
```

If you create a custom exception, it should inherit the type Error which gives the standard format with the minimum payload excepted. However, this is optional, and the exception mechanism will still work.

Like every language, an exception is only for an alternative path that occurs exceptionally. The reason is that exception flow is harder to understand and is not performant. There are alternatives possible. For example, the function in error can return an error object, or undefined. However, the return option has the drawback of taking the spot of potential returned value. It's possible to return the desired type and union with the exception type to mitigate the return scenario. Indeed, the union solution brings more type check on each invocation which might not be convenient. Another alternative to communicating exception is with a parameter that is a function callback invoked in case of error. Finally, a possible choice, in the case of code using promises, is to reject the promise.

The object sent by the exception into the catch clause can use "instanceOf" to narrow to a particular treatment depending on the type. However, a particularity to compare a type that inherits the base class Error is that every constructor must set the prototype to the actual class it belongs. The reason is that since TypeScript 2.1, the constructor function Error, Array, and Map doesn't propagate. The workaround is using the "setPrototypeOf" function in the constructor of each class in the hierarchy. The function sets the prototype to another object.

```
class ArgumentNullException extends Error {
   constructor(public name: string) {
      super("Argument was undefined");
      Object.setPrototypeOf(this, ArgumentNullException.prototype);
   }
}
class ReferenceException extends Error {
   constructor(public x: number, public y: number) {
      super("Reference was undefined");
      Object.setPrototypeOf(this, ReferenceException.prototype);
   }
}
function throwTwoExceptions(switcher: boolean) {
   if (switcher) {
      throw new ArgumentNullException("Switcher");
   }
   throw new ReferenceException(1, 2);
}
try {
   throw new ArgumentNullException("Switcher");
}
catch (ex) {
   if (ex instanceof ArgumentNullException) {
      console.log("I can access name:" + ex.name);
   } else if (ex instanceof ReferenceException) {
      console.log("I can access x and y:" + ex.x + " and " + ex.y);
   }
}
```

Exceptions are tricky when mixed with the concept of promise. It is best to avoid having an exception with asynchronous code. However, exceptions happen. In that case, the promise that has the exception thrown must use the "catch" directly at the promise's level without wrapping the promise in a try-catch statement. Promise doesn't have the concept of explicit "finally" clause. To mimic a final clause, the code needs a "then" clause after the "catch."

```
Promise.resolve("value to be in the argument of then")
  .then((response: string) => {
    throw new Error("Error message");
  })
  .then((response: string) => {
    console.log("Second then", response);
    return Promise.resolve(response);
  })
  .catch((err: Error) => {
    console.log("Error Message", err.message);
  })
  .then((response: string) => {
    console.log("Always called");
  })

// Error Message Error message
// Always called
```

The catch clause can omit the variable. The simplification removes the parentheses as well as the parameter. The reason for not using the exception is for situations where regardless of the reason, the code must always act the same way.

```
try{
  throw new Error("Error but doesn't care about
                   the exception or message");
} catch{
  console.log("Catch all exceptions without looking at the exception");
}
```

5.10 VARIANCE

TypeScript variances using the nomenclature of another language is confusing by nature. It's not something you must master since the compiler will stop you from doing something crazy. However, it's good to understand before having the compiler. Before getting started, let's create some interfaces to examine how TypeScript handles (or not) covariant, contravariant, bivariant and invariant type. We will create three interfaces which will be all inherited in the chain. So, InterfaceA inherits InterfaceB which inherits InterfaceC.

Let's start with **invariance**. It does accept supertype; it also does not accept subtype. With our three interfaces, if a function had the type InterfaceB, the only interface is acceptable. To have an invariant language, you need a sound language which TypeScript is not.

Covariance accepts supertype but not subtype. In our example, a function accepting type InterfaceB would only accept InterfaceB and InterfaceC. **Contravariance** is the opposite; it accepts the type and subtype. InterfaceA and InterfaceB would be accepted.

Finally, **bivariance** is the only remaining option which allows everything from the chain.

TypeScript uses covariance.

5.11 IN OPERATOR

The "in" operator can narrow a type from a union. The left part of the operand is a string or a string literal. The right part is a union type. The result is a Boolean that returns true if the union contains the string, and false if not.

```
interface IN_A { m1: number, m2: boolean };
interface IN_B { m3: string };

function foo(x: IN_A | IN_B) {
  if ("m1" in x) {
    console.log("Type narrowed to IN_A", x.m1, x.m2);
  } else {
    console.log("Type narrowed to IN_B", x.m3);
  }
  console.log("A is still IN_A or IN_B");
}
```

5.12 CONDITIONAL TYPE

TypeScript 2.8 brings the possibility of conditional type. Conditional type creates type by checking if an interface or an existing type extends a type or not. It uses the ternary operator to the final type. The following code shows a function that takes a type T for parameter. The generic T extends a union of two types. The returns type is a type that uses the condition type. The type accepts the two union values and applies a condition that swaps the two types. For example, in the code below, the dynamic type is a number because the "InterfaceChild" inherits "InterfaceBase", hence uses the first type.

```
interface InterfaceBase {
  method1(): void;
}
interface InterfaceChild extends InterfaceBase {
  method2(): void;
}

type DynamicTypeFromCond = InterfaceChild extends InterfaceBase ?
number : string;
```

5.13 INFER

TypeScript 2.8 brings a new keyword, "infer." The new addition returns a type from a generic. The role of infer is to tell TypeScript to figure out the type instead of defining the type at the class or function level. Normally, generic requires having the generic type from the start. However, in some situations, the type may not be known.

A use case of "infer" is when a type extends a function that returns an unknown type. It's possible to use "infer" to have the type be a generic variable.

```
type GetReturnedType<T> = T extends ((...args: any[]) => infer R) ? R : T;

function whatIsMyReturnType(): number {
  return 1;
}
// number from 'R'
type TypeFromReturn = GetReturnedType<typeof whatIsMyReturnType>;
const dynamicallyTyped: TypeFromReturn = 1;
// number from 'T'
type TypeFromReturn2 = GetReturnedType<number>;
```

In the previous code, the type "TypeFromReturn" gets the type using a type's helper that expects a generic type to be a function. The function returns "infer R." Before TypeScript 2.8, this would have been "any." However, now, it is possible to infer the type. The example leverages the conditional type. If the generic type is not a function, it returns the actual type. The second type, named "TypeFromReturn2", does not return the "R" but the "T" because it calls the "GetReturnedType" with a primitive instead of a function.

CHAPTER 6: ITERATORS

TypeScript brings many ECMAScript ways to loop through array or object implementing Symbol.iterator. In the area of iteration, nothing is unique to TypeScript.

6.1 KEY

The first way is to iterate the key of an object. Looping the key is the role of "for-in" loop. You can use for-in on a normal array. The result is a list of indexes which would be the sequential order of each element. On an object, you will iterate all members' names.

```
let list1: (number | string)[] = [1, 2, 3, "a", "b", "c"];
for (let i in list1) {
  console.log(i); // 0, 1, 2, 3, 4, 5
}
```

6.2 VALUE

The second way to iterate a collection is on the value of an object which is done using "for-of." Using it on an array will provide the value in the array. Doing it on an object will not work; for-of is more restrictive because it must implement Symbol.iterator. The difference is you cannot use this iteration mechanism on a literal object like you could do for-in.

```
let list2: (number | string)[] = [1, 2, 3, "a", "b", "c"];
for (let i of list2) {
  console.log(i); // 1, 2, 3, "a", "b", "c"
}
```

6.3 FOREACH

There is a short-end for a structure using Symbol.iterator which is to use the function "foreach." The parameter is the element inside the iterable structure. If you have an array of number, each result will be a number; if it's an array of object, it will be an object. The "foreach" also has a second parameter which is the index of the element in the array. The third parameter is the array itself. The last parameter is rarely used.

```
let list3: (number | string)[] = [1, 2, 3, "a", "b", "c"];
list3.forEach(
  (v: string | number,
    index: number,
    array: (string | number)[]
  ) => {
    console.log("Value " + v + " at position " + index);
  });
// Value 1 at position 0
// Value 2 at position 1
// Value 3 at position 2
// Value a at position 3
// Value b at position 4
// Value c at position 5
```

6.4 FOR AND WHILE

You can also loop with the standard "for" loop. Using an index works as well for an array, but again, it won't let you loop an object without using object.keys() or object.entries() which both returns array. For your information, the "entries" function requires using a lib called "es2017.object" that must be set in TypeScript compiler.

```
let listArrayPrimitive = {
  m1: "valuem1",
  m2: 2
};
const keys = Object.keys(listArrayPrimitive);
const entries = Object.entries(listArrayPrimitive); // require to have "lib": [
"es2017.object" ]

console.log("keys", keys);
console.log("entries", entries);

// keys [ 'm1', 'm2' ]
// entries [ [ 'm1', 'valuem1' ], [ 'm2', 2 ] ]
```

6.5 ASYNCHRONOUS LOOP

TypeScript generators is an advanced and very modern concept. It uses the function* syntax which is the standard "function" keyword followed by an asterisk. The star syntax indicates that a function returns a generator object. A function that returns a generator object can return multiple times. This function lets the use of the keyword "yield" which returns a value without returning the function. It allows to iterate potentially infinitely and still be able to consume the value outside the function. The function returns a generator object which has a ".next()" function. The next function returns a value of type IteratorResult. The function returns when the iteration is over with a "done" property from IteratorResult. The "done" is of type Boolean, and it tells a "while" or a "for" loop when to stop.

At the time I am writing these lines, it's still not straightforward to set up TypeScript to work with the async iterator. The first step is to change the tsconfig.json to have the library "esnext.asynciterator." The second step is to redefine the asynciterator with the "any" hack. The example needs to fake something that takes time which will be a delay function that returns a promise after a specific number of milliseconds. We also need a method to generate something every time the delay is over. For that example, we will generate a random set of string. The third step is to create the function* which yields returns value. The method can return a single value or an array. When yielding an array, a start must follow the "yield" keyword. In this example, to demonstrate both, the loop is yielding a single set of characters before the delay and two sets after in the array syntax. Finally, the function* must be invoked. You can refer to the following example at step 4, where we are looping the function*. The loop uses the keyword "await" to await the next yielded value.

```
// Step1
(<any>Symbol).asyncIterator = Symbol.asyncIterator
      || Symbol.for("Symbol.asyncIterator");
// Step 2
function delay(ms: number): Promise<void> {
  return new Promise<void>((resolve) => {
    setTimeout(resolve, ms);
  });
}
function getRandomSetChars(): string {
  const random = 1 + Math.floor(Math.random() * 5);
  let wordString = "";
  for (let i = 0; i < random; i++) {
    const letter = 97 + Math.floor(Math.random() * 26);
    wordString += String.fromCharCode(letter);
  }
  return wordString;
}
// Step 3
async function* getRandomSetsChars(): AsyncIterableIterator<string> {
  for (let i = 0; i < 10; i++) {
    yield getRandomSetChars(); // return a random set of char
    await delay(200); // wait
    yield* [getRandomSetChars(), getRandomSetChars()]; // return two
random sets of char
  }
}
// Step 4
async function addWordsAsynchronously() {
  for await (const x of getRandomSetsChars()) {
    console.log("Iterator loop:" + x);
  }
}
addWordsAsynchronously();
```

CHAPTER 7: COMPARISON

TypeScript inherited from JavaScript its laxity around comparison. As we saw earlier, TypeScript reduces potential JavaScript quirks by increasing the strictness. However, nothing forces developers to employ the triple equals which is key to avoid type conversion that occurs while using the double equals. TypeScript helps with the double equals by removing some edge cases. For example, comparing a number with a number in a string works fine in JavaScript but won't compile with TypeScript.

```
let value1String: string = "1";
let value1Number: number = 1;
if(value1String == value1Number){
  console.log("TypeScript doesn't compile");
}
```

7.1 VALUE & REFERENCE

Primitive compares by value. On the other hand, object literal, an object from classes, or array compares by reference.

```
const value1Object = { m1: "test" };
const value2Object = { m1: "test" };
if (value1Object === value2Object) {
  console.log("Should not print this line");
}
```

7.2 NULL & UNDEFINED

Null and undefined are different when compared with triple equals but are the same with double. In TypeScript, undefined is the type set for optional value and null for the explicit value describing that "nothing is set here." There is a trend of trying to rely on only undefined and avoid using null. However, you cannot take for granted that it is the case. There is a pattern to compare null or undefined, which is to look up for the variable without using operator. The lack of operator is problematic if the type is a number of a Boolean. For example, a Boolean may be undefined or false, and in both cases, it will fall into the same conditional statement. Confusing the value and the null or undefined might not be frequent, but codes tend to change. The return of a function could start with an object and end with a Boolean, which would still compile but change the behavior of how the code interprets the condition. In the end, being safe and using a few more keystrokes is the key to a resilient code, ideally using the triple equals to check for undefined and then for null (if both cases may apply).

The second scenario which requires fewer keystrokes is to use the double equals to null or undefined. In both cases, the verification tests the value of the object against null or undefined. It's still using the double equals but still better than just comparing to nothing and having the object or primitive converted to Boolean. An important configuration is to set "strictNullChecks" to true. The option in tsconfig.json will enforce a boundary between null and undefined.

```
let value2Boolean1: boolean | undefined = undefined;
let value2Boolean2: boolean | undefined = true;
let value2Boolean3: boolean | undefined = false;
if(!value2Boolean1){
  console.log("This is false 1");
}
if(!value2Boolean2){
  console.log("This is false 2");
}
if(!value2Boolean3){
  console.log("This is false 3");
}
// This is false 1
// This is false 3
```

These days, it's totally safe again to compare undefined with a triple equals sign. A long time ago, before ECMAScript 5, it was possible to redefine "undefined", hence not safe to compare against it directly. The redefine is why it was recommended to use "typeof" and to compare it against the string undefined. It's also possible to compare with a triple equals to void 0. The reason is that when the variable's value compared is undefined, it will equal to *void 0*. However, with TypeScript, the cleanest way to compare against undefined is to use the triple equals against the variable "undefined" directly.

```
const x: string | undefined = undefined;
if (x === undefined) { console.log("x undefined"); }
if (typeof x === "undefined") { console.log("x typeof undefined"); }
if (x === void 0) { console.log("x void 0"); }
```

7.3 OBJECTS COMPARISON

TypeScript uses structural typing and not nominal. It means that types are compared to its structure and not to the name of the interface or class or type. Popular languages like C# or Java are nominal, as well as the alternative language similar to TypeScript called Flow. Nominal comparison is a design-time-only comparison because JavaScript doesn't have types. TypeScript removes all types, hence cannot have code to compare against type name at run-time. In contrast, structural comparison, like TypeScript performs, are available at design and run-time.

We already covered how to do type checking with "typeof" and "instanceof." However, the comparison details on how flexible TypeScript remain. TypeScript doesn't allow to provide the exact type and be able to pass a comparison check. The importance is to respect the structure behind the type. The emphasis on the structure allows using any structure that respects the minimum similar fields but could pass more. For example, if there is a function that requires a parameter of the interface named "A" with a definition of a single member named "B," you could pass any interface or type or literal object that has a member named "B" with the same type as the original interface.

```
interface ParameterType { m1: number }
interface NotRelatedType { m1: number, m2: string, m3: boolean }
interface NotRelatedTypeNoM1Number { m1: string }

const i1: ParameterType = { m1: 1 };
const i2: NotRelatedType = { m1: 1, m2: "1", m3: true };
const i3: NotRelatedTypeNoM1Number = { m1: "1" };

function IWantParameterType(p: ParameterType): void { }
IWantParameterType(i1);
IWantParameterType(i2);
IWantParameterType(i3); // Doesn't compile
```

CHAPTER 8: FUNCTIONS

Functions are at the core of JavaScript. The language is function-scoped. TypeScript doesn't do any change in this regard and embraces the use of a class to delimit the scope, which is also a feature of ECMAScript 2015. In this chapter, we will review how we can define functions in TypeScript and draw the parallel in JavaScript. We will see how TypeScript enhances functions by providing a strong signature that defines parameters and the return type. We will see the outline of the "this" pointer which is often confused but simplified with TypeScript.

8.1 DEFINITION

The keyword "function" followed by the name of the function defines a new function. "Named function" is the explicit use of "function" to identify a function. With the same keyword, you can create an anonymous function which doesn't have a name. The anonymous function can use a variable for future invocation. In both cases, the function can be used multiple times and return a single value. TypeScript is not different than JavaScript in what concerns the scope of the variable consumed in a function. By that, it means that a function can access all defined functions within the function as well as all the ones outside of any parent scope. Functions can be imbricated, which creates a whole set of possibilities around encapsulation strategy. For example, you can have a function that has two functions. These two children functions can access the main function variables but cannot access each other's inner variables because both functions create a boundary since they are sibling scopes and not parent ones.

8.2 ANONYMOUS FUNCTION

TypeScript extends the concept of type to function's arguments. Types at the arguments level are valid for named functions and anonymous functions. Adding type to a function's argument is similar to how we specify the type of a variable, which is by using the colon character after the variable name. TypeScript supports return type. The function's return type uses the colon after the ending parenthesis of the function but before the curly brace. The returns type works the same as for a variable and can be of a primitive type, an interface or a union of many types.

When typing an anonymous function, you can opt to use the short version which uses the fat arrow symbol to specify the return type followed by the equal sign to define the function. We will talk more about fat arrow function soon.

8.3 FAT ARROW

The arrow function has been introduced with ECMAScript 6 and is another way to define a function. It reduces the number of keystrokes by removing the keyword "function" at the expense of using the equal sign followed by the greater than sign. The nomenclature is to open the parenthesis, define all parameters, close the parameter, use the fat arrow, open the curly brace and write the code of the function then close the curly brace finally. The position after the closing parenthesis between the colon and the fat arrow with the colon contains the return type.

```
const fatarrow = (p: number): number => { return number * 100; }
```

Other than brevity, the arrow syntax carries the reference for the "this" keyword from the parent context where the function is created. This is a huge improvement since before you had to create a temporary variable that was assigned to "this" before creating the function, and then instead of using this, to use the variable. Without doing this gymnastic, the "this" could be different depending on how the function was invoked, which may change easily, causing fickleness.

8.4 INFERENCE

Type inference is a way for TypeScript to figure out by itself the type of a type without having the developer to explicitly define the type. With version 2.1, TypeScript uses inference for every variable without a type. Before 2.1, TypeScript was assigning "any" instead of figuring the best type.

8.4.1 VARIABLE

TypeScript can infer the type of a variable and hence it is possible to avoid using the colon for anonymous function by simply setting the variable to an unnamed function which has typed parameters and return type. In the example below, all the "myAnonymous…" functions have no type defined but they are all strongly typed by inference.

```
const inc = 1;
function myNamedFunction(p: number): number { return p + inc; }
const myAnonymousFunc = function (p: number): number { return p + inc; }
const myAnonymousFunc2 = (p: number): number => { return p + inc; }
const myAnonymousFunc3 = (p: number): number => p + inc;
const myAnonymousFunc4 = (p: number) => p + inc;
```

In the case of function inside an interface, the name of a parameter doesn't need to match the definition and the function body of the implementation, only the type.

String, numeric and Boolean literal types were not inferred; they needed an explicit declaration with a colon. Starting with TypeScript 2.1, literal types are always inferred for const variables and read-only properties.

```
const infHello: "hello" = "hello"; // Explicit
const infWord = "world"; // Implicit using inference to "world"

let infHello2: "hello" = "hello"; // Explicit
let infWord2 = "world"; // Implicit using inference to string

let worldString: string = "world";

let windeningToString: string = infHello; // Compile because of windening
let narrowingToWorld: "world" = worldString; // Doesn't compile
```

8.4.2 GENERIC RETURN TYPE

TypeScript, since version 2.4, can infer the type of a function return.

```
function arrayMap<T, U>(f: (x: T) => U): (a: T[]) => U[] {
   return a => a.map(f);
}
const lengths: (a: string[]) => number[] = arrayMap(s => s.length);
```

Before version 2.4, the “s.length” was an error. The “s” was not from U[] type but an empty object literal {}.

8.5 OPTIONAL PARAMETERS

TypeScript lets you have optional parameter from different syntax. The first way is by using a union to specify the type of the argument and the type undefined. The second is to use the question mark operator after the parameter name and before the semi-colon. In the case of using the question mark, any subsequent argument must also be optional. The following argument cannot be of type undefined or null or a specific type without being optional. The reason is that optional has the feature of not needing to specify the parameter at invocation while the union with undefined still requires the user to pass undefined. A standard check against undefined is needed to figure out if the argument is optional or if undefined is assigned. It is not possible to distinguish between optional or undefined because both use the same comparison.

```
function undefinedOptional1(a: number | undefined, b: number) {
}
undefinedOptional1(undefined, 1);

function undefinedOptional2F(a?: number, b: number) {
// Doesn't compile because a is using optional: ?
}
undefinedOptional2F(); // Doesn't compile because of b is after a the optional
function undefinedOptional3F(a: number, b: number | undefined) { }
undefinedOptional3F(a); // Doesn't compile, must pass for "b" undefined if not needed
```

8.6 DEFAULT VALUE

Another feature is to have a default value for one of the parameters. Again, the syntax leverages existing knowledge, which is to use the single equal sign to set a variable to the argument. One difference is that you can set the default at every position in the signature. The reason is that contrary to the optional scenario, the default argument is always a value. The type is optional since TypeScript can infer it from the assignation which is always present for default, but it's still a good practice to make it explicit. With default parameter, the function uses the value when it doesn't receive any value from the invoker. The second case is when the function receives the value undefined.

```
function funcWithDefault(
    p1: string = "v1"
  , p2?: number
  , p3 = true) {
     console.log("P1", p1); // v1 since undefined
     console.log("P2", p2); // undefined
     console.log("P3", p3); //boolean by inference
  }

funcWithDefault(undefined);
// P1 v1
// P2 undefined
// P3 true
```

8.7 CLASS FUNCTION

Functions written inside a class are a little bit different. In the next chapter, we will talk about object-oriented and all the richer possibilities that TypeScript brings. In short, functions are similar but don't use the keyword "function." Instead, the explicit visibility of the function is used or even nothing.

8.8 THIS & FUNCTION EXPRESSION

TypeScript has the capability of letting the author of a function specify the type of "this." Without it, even with the arrow function, this may be of type "any." The lack of the type on "this" often occurs if you are using an object literal that had a function that returns a function that uses "this." The function in the object literal is called function expression, and returns "any" type when the value is accessed with "this." However, we know, as the author does, that the type means the object literal, hence can specify to TypeScript the type of this one. The syntax is to use "this" followed by a colon symbol followed by the expected type as the first parameter of the function signature.

```
interface MyThisInterface {
   m1: string[];
   m2: number[];
   functionA(): () => string;
}

let vMyThisInterface: MyThisInterface = {
   m1: ["hearts", "spades", "clubs", "diamonds"],
   m2: [1, 2, 3],
   functionA: function () {
      return () => {
         return this.m1[0]; // This is any
      }
   }
}

vMyThisInterface.functionA();
```

Can be changed to:

```
interface MyThisInterface {
  m1: string[];
  m2: number[];
  functionA(this: MyThisInterface): () => string;
}

let vMyThisInterface: MyThisInterface = {
  m1: ["hearts", "spades", "clubs", "diamonds"],
  m2: [1, 2, 3],
  functionA: function (this: MyThisInterface) {
    return () => {
      return this.m1[0];
    }
  }
}

vMyThisInterface.functionA();
```

You can also block the usage of "this" by using the same technic of specifying the type; however, this time with "void" instead of the type.

Often, the reference of "this" is lost when a function takes a callback function. By default, "this" refers to the context of which the function is called.

```
const family = {
  names: ["Patrick", "Alicia", "Melodie"],
  emotion: "love",
  print: function () {
    console.log("print", this); // this = the family object
    return this.names.forEach(function (name: string) {
      console.log("forEach", this); // this = Node.js
    });
  }
};
family.print();
```

In the example above, the first console.log prints the family object, but the second, inside the "forEach" function, is bound to the caller which is

Node.js environment when executed from the command line or windows when executed from the browser. To solve this issue, using the fat arrow function will set this to the parent who is the family object. This solution is elegant in terms of its short syntax size and also avoids setting the value of this which would be required if using other solutions available before ECMAScript 2015 like using "bind" or passing this when the function allows setting the value of it by the parameter.

```
return this.names.forEach((name: string) => {});
return this.names.forEach(function(name: string) {}.bind(this));
return this.names.forEach(function(name: string) {}, family);
```

8.9 NO EXPLICIT RETURN TYPE

Functions can return an implicit type or an explicit type. By default, TypeScript returns a void type. However, if not specified and the code returns a number, the return type would implicitly be a number. If later the function returns a string, what is the expected return value? The lack of clarity can lead to confusion while having the flexibility of returning an array of potential types. It is possible to return more than a single type by using a union and still restrict potential return type. The unpredictability of the return type is the reason why having an explicit return type is always a better practice than relying on inference. The explicit mention of the type defines a clear contract that cannot change without altering the return type manually.

```
function withImplicitReturnType(b:boolean){
  if(b){
    return 10;
  }
  return "test";
}
```

The example above returns the implicit type of 10 unions the string literal "test".

8.10 OVERLOADED FUNCTION

TypeScript allows having an overload of a function. Often, the term overload is linked to an object-oriented concept which we will see later. Any functions, even if not in a class, can have overload. The reason to use overload function is that you may have a function that takes some required parameters only in a specific scenario. Instead of using overloaded function, it's possible to use optional parameter and default parameter. The advantage of overloaded function is clarity for the consumer. From the consumer perspective, this one will see several functions with different signatures (parameters and return type). However, it's still a single function.

Overload embraces the principle of overloading beyond not just parameter but also with the return type. Overloading is quite useful since without overload you wouldn't know which group of optional parameters belong together and which of them match which returns type. Using overload requires having several functions with the same name defined next to each other with a body. That's right, a signature from the keyword function to the return type that ends up with a semi-colon. Only the last defined function requires being more conventional with a full body. This last one must contain the aggregation of all overload. For example, if you have an overload that takes a number and returns a number, and the second one that takes a string and returns a string, the last definition will contain a signature with a single parameter that unites a number and a string with a return type of number union string. This one will handle all function overloads which means that you will see at the beginning of the function code that it will assess if specific parameters are defined and act accordingly. Other than providing a clear idea of what parameters amongst optional and with what return type they are associated, overload syntax makes the Intellisense richer with IDE that can separate the scenarios with proper documentation and possible combination of syntax.

```
function functionWithOverload(param1: number): boolean;
function functionWithOverload(param1: number, param2: string): string;
function functionWithOverload(
  param1: number
```

```
    , param2: string = "default"
    , param3?: string): boolean | string {
    if (param3 === undefined) {
        return "string";
    }
    return true;
}
```

8.11 STRING LITERAL AND OVERLOAD

A function can use a string literal in its parameter to know which return type is possible. For example, it's possible to have a function with a string parameter and have many overloads where a specific string value will sway to code into one or the other function. In the example below, the method accepts only the string "batman" and "superman" even if the signature shows string. TypeScript unites both overloads to create a string literal of all the overloads. For example, if you are using an IDE that supports TypeScript, the IDE will show the return type Batman if the parameter is "batman."

```
interface SuperHero { }
interface Batman extends SuperHero { }
interface SuperMan extends SuperHero { }

function createSuperHero(name: "batman"): Batman;
function createSuperHero(name: "superman"): SuperMan;
function createSuperHero(name: string): SuperHero {
    if (name === "batman") { return {}; }
    else if (name === "superman") { return {}; }
    return {};
}
```

8.12 VOID

There is a caveat with function-and-return type. A function that has a signature that returns void and returns a number won't fail. It returns more than required, hence will pass the compilation check. A common usage of the caveat is that you may have a framework code that expects to have a callback function of void and you provide a callback that returns an object.

The value returned is discarded.

8.13 FUNCTION WITH PARAMETER FUNCTION

A function's signature can have a parameter that is a function too. These function's parameter can have parameters at their turn but doesn't require the invoker to use the parameters. A standard scenario is for the optional callback function. For example, say you have a function that lets you specify an optional error callback named "error" of type "Error." Not using the argument occurs when the notification by the callback is important, but not the detail from the argument. The reason is that behind it, JavaScript provides the value. The inspection of the "arguments" object, when not using the argument, corroborates this assertion. However, since you are not using the value, there is no need to clutter the code. TypeScript works in this dynamic fashion because of JavaScript. Since it doesn't generate any potential error, TypeScript doesn't enforce an unnecessary check.

```
function functParams(p1: string, err: (e: Error) => void): void {}

functParams("test", () => { }); // Parameter e:Error not required
functParams("test", (whatEver:Error) => { }); // Name can be changed
functParams("test", (e:Error) => { });
```

8.14 FUNCTION AND INFINITE ARGUMENTS

Functions can take an undefined number of parameters with the rest operator. The rest operator is three dots before the name of the parameter. An array of any type can use the rest operator. Only the last parameter of a function can use the rest operator. Every parameter beyond the ones provided before the rest will fall into this variable. We could accomplish something similar by specifying an optional array which would force the consumer of the function to create an array and set the parameters. However, with a rest parameter, you can, as the consumer, write parameters just like any parameter with a comma between the value passed.

```
function functRest(p1: string, ...remaining: string[]): void { }
functRest("p1", "p2", "p3");

function functBefore(p1: string, remaining: string[]): void { }
functBefore("p1", ["p2", "p3"]);
```

8.15 FUNCTION CALLBACK

A function that has a parameter that is a callback which returns nothing, to be void, can have a function returning a value. The compilation is successful because it provides more than expected. TypeScript does not do anything with the returned value and believes it's void while underneath it will have the value.

For example, if you have a function that accepts a callback function and that you pass a function that returns an object, a number or an array or a string, it will compile. The following example shows that the callback expects a void return. However, the function calls with a callback that returns a string. As you can see below, specifying the type void to a function doesn't protect the consumer of the callback to read the return value. This concept doesn't extend beyond the return type void. For example, if the callback expects to return a string, you won't be able to use a function that returns a number -- "void" is a special case.

```
function functReturnVoid(f: () => void): void {
   const c: void = f();
   console.log(c); // Print the string
}
functReturnVoid(() => { return "I am a string, not void!" }); // Callback !void
```

CHAPTER 9: OBJECT-ORIENTED

In this chapter, we will see how to create objected-oriented code with TypeScript. ECMAScript is getting up-to-date by allowing more and more codes to borrow the concept of object-oriented. TypeScript simplifies the process by bringing strong type around object-oriented. Also, TypeScript transpiles modern object-oriented to an older version of ECMAScript that doesn't support it. When transpiling into a lower version of ECMAScript, TypeScript uses function closure tricks (IIFE) and optimizes the use of the function's prototype. Otherwise, at a higher ECMAScript version that supports class, TypeScript outputs a very similar code in JavaScript, but without type.

At the core of the object-oriented paradigm is the class. A class is a fundamental difference between the coding paradigm of JavaScript which is the function. However, both of them have something similar, i.e. they circumscribe specific members like variables and functions into a limited area of propagation.

9.1 CLASS

TypeScript defines classes by using the keyword "class" followed by the name that they will be referenced later once instantiated. A class contains members that have a modifier, also known as visibility.

A class should never be empty. Having an empty class opens the door to assigning everything, except undefined and null which is like a wild card. Also, two classes can have the same members, which means they are not unique in terms of their structure. To make two classes different, only a difference in a private member is enough even if they have the same name. For example, if you have class "A" and class "B" defined with the same structure, they can swap. The swap means that a variable of type "B" can accept a variable of type "A." Also, if "B" has the same structure as "A" but with more members, it will also work. Here is an example that illustrates the last scenario.

```
// Empty class
class ClassEmpty { }
function functionEmptyClass(c: ClassEmpty) { }
functionEmptyClass({ m1: "" });

// Interchangeable if structure the same
class ClassInterchangeable1 { m1: string };
class ClassInterchangeable2 { m1: string; m2: string };
function functionInterchangeable(c: ClassInterchangeable1) { }
functionInterchangeable(new ClassInterchangeable2());
```

9.2 ACCESS MODIFIER

The modifier can be public, private, or protected. By default, everything is public, which means that once the class instantiated it will be available. The availability of the variable is different with the public counterpart private.

Private members are only accessible within the class. The goal of setting members private is to create an encapsulation which gives you some freedom to reduce the exposition to the only significant element of a concept. Furthermore, field members may require validations and hence require to pass through to specific code to be assigned. A private modifier restrains direct access to the variable. The restriction forces a change in value into a controlled flow by limiting access to public functions.

For the protected access modifier, the visibility makes members available only for the class and in the inheritance chain. A class "A" that inherits a second class "B" that inherits the third class "C" will expose its protected members to "B" and "A" while "B"-protected members will be accessible by itself and by "A."

```
class ClassModifier {
  public m1: string;
  protected m2: string;
  private m3: string;
}
class ClassModifier2 extends ClassModifier{
  public m4: string;
  protected m5: string;
  private m6: string;
  private m7():void{
    this.m1;
    this.m2;
    // m3 is not accessible
  }
}
const classModified = new ClassModifier();
classModified.m1; // Only member available
const classModifier2 = new ClassModifier2();
classModifier2.m1; // 1/2 member available
classModifier2.m4; // 2/2 member available
```

Protected accessor brings trust in the hierarchy and protects access from outside this one.

9.3 CONSTRUCTOR

The class has the concept of the constructor. The instantiation of a class calls the constructor. You can see the constructor has a special function. To specify which function the constructor has, it needs to use the reserved keyword "constructor" instead of a custom name. A class can only have a single constructor, which can have as many parameters as desired. A constructor is optional and only required in particular situations.

The first situation where a constructor is interesting is when you would like to assign values to the creation of an object. Setting variables in the constructor enforces value into required fields. The second situation is when you have inheritance, and the base class has a constructor. The only way to call the base constructor is to have a child class having a constructor. The second case will be covered in a few when exposing the inheritance in

TypeScript.

```
class ClassWithConstrutor {
  public m1: string;
  public constructor() {
    this.m1 = "Initial value";
  }
}
```

A constructor can be private. Private constructor prevents instantiation from outside the class with the keyword "new." Private constructor means creating an instance only from inside the class often results in a public static method. The static method is public and accessible from the class itself to create an instance.

```
class PrivateConstructor {
  private constructor() { }
  public static getNewInstance(): PrivateConstructor {
    return new PrivateConstructor();
  }
}
const pc1 = new PrivateConstructor(); // Doesn't compile
const pc2 = PrivateConstructor.getNewInstance();
```

9.4 INHERITANCE

We introduced with the modifier "protected" the inheritance behavior that class can benefit from. Inheritance is a core concept of object-oriented where a class can extend another class. With TypeScript, a class can extend only a single class. Once done, the subclass that inherits the base class can access public and protected members of the base class. In terms of consumption, when a type is required, you can use the exact type or a subtype. The reason is that the subtype fulfills the contract of the type requested by providing all members of the contract but also more. Often, the term "superclass" is for the base class. Subclass constructor must call the superclass by using the keyword "super" with all required parameters of the superclass. For example, if the base class requires having a string, the subclass may or may not have a constructor with a parameter but for sure requires to call the super function with a string. The call of "super" can be anywhere in the constructor but before any use of "this." The keyword "super" can be used if you need a reference to the base class. While the right way to access is to use "this" which gives you access to the current class as well as the base class, the keyword super is handy to ensure you are accessing the right member when two members borrow the same name.

```
class SuperClass {
  constructor(p1: number) { }
}
class ChildClass extends SuperClass {
  constructor(p2: number, p3: string) {
    super(p2);
  }
}
const c = new ChildClass(1, "3");
```

A variable can use the type of a class like any primitives, types, or interfaces. The usage is to write, after a colon, the name of the class. The class as a type is good for parameters and variables. The difference among primitive, type, or interface is with the class you must instantiate with the "new" keyword. After "new", the exact type or any subtype that inherits the desired type is written. TypeScript compares classes structurally, like interfaces, but with a minor difference. Private and protected members must come from the same class. The detail around private and protected means that if you have two classes with the same structure, which also have the same private members, it will result in two different entities during the comparison.

```
class ClassInterchangeable3 { public m1: string; private p1: number; };
class ClassInterchangeable4 { public m2: string; private p1: number; };

function functionPrivateStructure(p: ClassInterchangeable3) { }
functionPrivateStructure(new ClassInterchangeable3());
functionPrivateStructure(new ClassInterchangeable4()); // Doesn't compile
```

9.5 PARAMETER PROPERTIES

A parameter property is a way to declare and set values to members during the construction phase. A parameter property takes out the burden of having to declare the variable as a member of the class and to set the value from the parameter of the constructor to the members. Parameter properties is a shortcut that lets you declare the variable and set its value directly in the constructor signature. To be able to use this shortcut, the constructor must specify the visibility of the member, the name of the variable, and the type. The constructor's signature can mingle between property initializer and standard parameter.

```
class ClassParameterProperty {
  constructor(public m1: string, m2: string) { }
}
const cpp = new ClassParameterProperty("asd", "qwe");
cpp.m1; // Available
cpp.m2; // Not available
```

9.6 STATIC

A non-static function defined in classes written with a version of ECMAScript before 6 will transpile into functions set in the prototype chain of a literal object. However, a variable function or a non-static function transforms into a variable function of the literal object created. The generated prototype function is shared with all consumers of the object literal like the static function does. From ECMAScript 6, static is supported directly into the class.

```
// Es5 and lower
var StaticClass = /** @class */ (function () {
  function StaticClass() {
  }
  StaticClass.aStaticFunction = function () {
    console.log("This is called from a static function");
  };
  return StaticClass;
}());

// Es2017
class StaticClass {
  static aStaticFunction() {
    console.log("This is called from a static function");
  }
}
```

In TypeScript, a class cannot be static. The reason is that there is not a lot of advantage since you can define functions and variables directly into a module and use it.

9.7 THIS

There's still some issue with the pointer "this" when using event callback attached to a listener; for example, if you want a function in a class to handle the mouse on an HTML page. If you set the function of your class, any use of "this" will be assigned to "window." The problem is that most of the time, the desired behavior is to have "this" to the class where the function is defined. To solve this issue, we can use the fat arrow function, but in some cases, this might not be the right approach since it might create multiple assignations depending on where you set up the listener to the event. One popular approach is to wrap the function in the constructor by assigning a function of the class with "bind." The "bind" wraps the actual function with a function that has "this" assigned to the parameter passed in the bind, where you should pass "this." In this section, we will see the pros and cons of each approach.

```
class ClassThis {
  constructor() {
    this.eventFunction2 = this.eventFunction2.bind(this);
  }
  private instanceFunction = () => { };
  public attachEvents(): void {
    window.addEventListener("mousedown", this.eventFunction); // #1
    window
      .addEventListener("mouseup", (e) => this.eventFunction(e)); // #2
    window.addEventListener("mouseleave", this.eventFunction2); // #3
    window.addEventListener("mouseout", this.instanceFunction); // #4
  }
  private eventFunction(e: MouseEvent) { }
  private eventFunction2(e: MouseEvent) { }
}
```

In the code above, the commented line #1 is problematic since it invokes "this" with the "this" of the object "window." An event listener is not the only example where "this" can go rogue and act differently than expected. Like event listeners, many promise resolution, library callbacks or binding function event. TypeScript uses JavaScript and "this" is not an exception to the rule. It means that "this" is hard to wrap our head around. A few steps can clarify how to determine the value of this which will lead us to discuss solutions for further details. The first rule is that if the function "bind" got used to assign "this", then "this" is the one specified at the first parameter of the "bind" function. This rule is simple because it is very explicit. The second rule is that if the function calls a function using the instance of a class, "this" will refer to the instance of the class. This rule is true with class created with the "new" keyword but also class method created from object literal. In all other cases, "this" is assigned to "window" when executed from a browser, or the global environment when using Nodejs. Most of the time, the latter case is identifiable by using a function without parentheses, without executing the function.

Comment #2 in the example above identifies the first solution, and it uses the fat arrow. The fat arrow is a good solution for many reasons. It's easy to type; it is type safe, doesn't require any code other than where the callback/event requires the function. However, nothing is perfect. This approach has to pass the parameter down from the callback/event to the instance function and it creates a new function, hence could add overhead in memory.

The second solution is to use "bind." As mentioned, "bind" is the explicit way to assign "this." What it does behind the scene creates a reference that keeps a reference of "this" and calls "apply" with the first parameter of the "bind" function. It's safe to use but should be used wisely, which means that you must do it once and not on an area of code that does it several times. The unique identification is the reason this assignation is mostly inside a class constructor. Other than the clarity of what "this" will be, this solution has the advantage that when binding you do not need to pass the parameters like the fat arrow solution. However, you need to pass the "this" twice which is to select the function from the class and pass the class to the "this" parameter of a bind. Also, the "bind" function is only available since ECMAScript 5.

The third solution is to call a variable that holds the function instead of a class function. The variable solution is called "instance function." The result creates a single closure with the fat arrow around the actual code that will have "this" as the class reference. The advantage is that it's type safe with TypeScript and, like "bind" parameters that are automatically bound, requires less to type. It's also not possible to alter the "this" as you could do with "bind." "this" is always the instance where the variable lives. Indeed, the main disadvantage is the additional closure per method per instance. It is still more advantageous than creating the closure on every invocation with the fat arrow.

9.8 READONLY

Classes with a visibility modifier allow controlling how members are exposed. There is an additional way to harness the member type of variable which is with the "readonly" modifier. The goal of read-only is to allow the value to be dynamically assigned but not changed once set. There are two different assignations available with read-only, i.e. while declaring or inside the constructor. The parameter properties can use read-only as well. Types and interfaces can mention read-only to their members.

```
class WithReadonly {
   public readonly x: number = 3;
   public constructor(public readonly y: number = 4){
      this.x = 1; // Not required, but work
      this.y = 5; // Not required, but work
   }
   private funct():void{
      // this.x = 3; // Won't compile
   }
}
```

A type, interface, or class that has all its attributes read-only can only assign values at creating. A full read-only definition can be a step toward an object that is immutable where every modification requires creating a new instance. However, be aware that read-only is a concept that is applied at design time and removed at runtime, which means that the immutability is theoretical and doesn't extend beyond the realm of TypeScript. If you are building an application in TypeScript, this may be sufficient, but if you are building a third-party library and the output shared is in JavaScript, then it might require an additional library to achieve a pure immutable design.

```
interface ReadOnlyInterface {
   readonly x: number;
   readonly y: string;
}
const roi1: ReadOnlyInterface = {}; // Doesn't compile
const roi2: ReadOnlyInterface = {
   x: 1,
   y: "2"
};
```

Index signature can also be marked as read-only. The goal behind read-only and index signature is to allow accessing a value with the square bracket on an object but not allow setting any value.

```
interface ReadonlyCustomMap {
   readonly [index: string]: { message: string }
}

const map: ReadonlyCustomMap = {
   "a": { message: "b" }
};
console.log(map["a"]);
map["b"] = "b"; // Doesn't compile
```

9.9 ACCESSOR

Object-oriented has the notion of getter and setting, commonly named "accessor." Accessors are available, but not as used as having a public variable in a class. However, accessors provide a good way to provide validation when a value is set to a field or format data when consumed. There are some limitations with accessors. Accessors are only available if the output is to ECMAScript 5 and above. It is also automatically set to read-only if only a getter is provided and not a setter.

```
class ClassWithAccessor {
   private _privateMember: string;
   private _privateMember2: string;

   get privateMember(): string {
      return this._privateMember;
   }

   set privateMember(newName: string) {
      this._privateMember = newName;
   }
   get privateMember2(): string {
      return this._privateMember2;
   }
}
const cwa = new ClassWithAccessor();
cwa.privateMember = "Value";
cwa.privateMember2 = "Value"; // Doesn't compile
console.log(cwa.privateMember);
console.log(cwa.privateMember2);
```

9.10 ABSTRACT

The concept abstract comes from the object-oriented paradigm. The author of a class may write "abstract" before the keyword "class" to mark the class as abstract. By doing so, the class becomes a base class which cannot be instantiated alone. It requires a subclass to extend this one because every abstract member (variables or functions) must be defined in the subclass. That's right; an abstract class dictates what member must be present in the subclass. The abstract class can invoke the abstract members of its members. You can see abstract class as a mix of interface and class, with the advantage of being able to define logic that invokes or consumes members with a known signature but without knowing the implementation. Members can be abstract inside an abstract class. By marking a member abstract, this one cannot have specified visibility. In fact, when defining the member in the class that extends the abstract class, all members must be public. An abstract class can have public, private, or protected members like a normal class.

```
abstract class ClassAbstract {
   abstract member1: string;
   abstract function1(): string;

}

class ClassExtendAbstract extends ClassAbstract {
   member1: string; // This is public
   public function1(): string {
      return "f1";
   }
}

const abstObj1 = new ClassAbstract(); // Doesn't compile
const abstObj2 = new ClassExtendAbstract();
```

9.11 INTERFACE

Interfaces are used with object-oriented but also as a way to define a contract for object literal in TypeScript. Interfaces are similar to type, but with more features that we will define soon. It's important to understand that interfaces don't translate into JavaScript. It's purely a concept that Typescript handles to help the author of TypeScript to define a contract that must be respected when defining classes or when moving data around. Without interfaces and types, it would be possible to define a contract for an object by using inline annotation, which means that after the colon to use the curly bracket and specify desired members. However, this is not reusable and doesn't allow to leverage interface feature. One of its features is that interface can be declared in many places which allows anyone to enhance a contract at any time, even if the project defines the interface outside the project.

```
const withoutTypeOrInt: { x: number } = { x: 1 };
interface Int1 { x: number }
const withInterface: Int1 = { x: 1 };
```

Interfaces are open-ended in TypeScript to stay in the spirit of flexibility that JavaScript procures.

```
interface InterfaceDefinition1 {
  x: number;
}
interface InterfaceDefinition1 {
  y: number;
}
const interfaceMerged: InterfaceDefinition1 =
  { x: 1, y: 2 };
```

Classes can implement the interface by using the keyword "implements" after the class name. If the class extends another class, the "implements" must take place after the extends. Contrary to extends, implementing lets you define as many interfaces as you wish. An interface lets you define optional properties by using the question mark after the name of the property. The question mark indicates that the property may be provided or not. It helps to shape the type with potential members without having to be too much flexible and allowing everything.

```
interface InterfaceIA { ia: number; }
interface InterfaceIB { ib: number; }
class ClassWithImplementA
   implements InterfaceIA {
   public ia: number;

}
class ClassWithImplementB
   extends ClassWithImplementA
   implements InterfaceIB {
   public ib: number;
}
```

An interface lets you use the read-only modifier which enforces a single value to be set during initialization and for the rest of the life of the object that implements the interface.

Interfaces support indexable type. To define one, you must use the square bracket, the name of the index followed by a colon and the type which can be number or string, closing with the square bracket, semi-colon and the type expected to be pushed in the index. It's important to note that the index of a number must be a subtype of the same type as the string's index because at the end, in JavaScript, both are converted into a string. Indexable type is perfect for creating an arbitrary number of properties which can be the case when doing a hashmap structure. Combining with a read-only, you can create a read-only structure that can have data assigned at creation and only accessible to read in consumption. One caveat of the indexable type is that if you have defined a return type of string, you will only be able to define the normal property of type string. For example, you cannot have a variable named "lastUpdated" of type "Date." The string constraint is a constraint of JavaScript that any members are available as an index as well.

```
interface InterfaceMap {
  [id: string]: string;
  m1: string;
  // m2: Date; // Doesn't compile, must be string!
}

const im1: InterfaceMap = { m1: "Member" };
im1.m1 = "Member2";
im1["m1"] = "Member3";
im1["m2"] = "Member4";
console.log("Dictionary Values", im1);
// Dictionary Values { m1: 'Member3', m2: 'Member4' }
```

An interface can extend many interfaces. Multiple interfaces are useful if you want to reuse interface or break down into smaller cohesive groups but still be able to group them in a specific situation. For example, if you are using React which passes specific property interface that defines which properties you can use for a component, you can leverage the characteristic of many extends. You can have the component's property extend the dispatch actions, and the property extends the data model that contains the variables to display. The main advantage is that in many places in the application you may need only the data model, and in others the actions, which you can still pass since you have three distinct interfaces.

```
interface InterfaceHierarchical1 {
  m1: string;
}
interface InterfaceHierarchical2 extends InterfaceHierarchical1 {
  m2: string;
}
const ih1: InterfaceHierarchical2 = {
  m1: "m1",
  m2: "m2"
};
```

One last feature related to an interface being able to extend other interfaces is that an interface can extend a class. Extending class is unusual if we compare to other languages and rarely used in practice. By extending a class, TypeScript will extract all members that are public, protected, and private and will ignore the implementation and constructor.

```
class ClassThatWillBeExtended {
   m1: string;
   constructor() { }
   private m2(): void { }
   public m3(): void { }
}
interface InterfaceThatExtendsClass extends ClassThatWillBeExtended {
   m1: string;
}
```

One best practice is never to define an interface with an empty body. The reason is that it will allow to pass every type (even primitive) but not null or undefined which differs slightly from using the type any. It's still very wide open, which can lead to a multitude of anomalies.

```
interface WideOpen { }
function f(p: WideOpen) { }
f(1);
f({ z: 1 });
f(null); // Doesn't compile
f(undefined) // Doesn't compile
```

The keyword type and interface are very similar. The official documentation is obsolete concerning a few topics. For example, since version 2.1, TypeScript shows in the error message the actual interface name or the type name instead of the structure it defines. This is helpful because it links to the actual type. Another misconception is that only an interface can extend a class or an interface but not a type. Actually, a bot can do it.

```
type TypeToExtends { x: number };
interface InterfaceToExtends { x: number };

class ClassImplementsInterface implements InterfaceToExtends {x: number}
class ClassImplementsType implements TypeToExtends { x: number }
interface InterfaceExtendsInterface extends InterfaceToExtends {x: number}
interface InterfaceExtendsType extends TypeToExtends { x: number }
```

A difference is that a type cannot extend an interface. Combining a type requires the use of an intersection. Often, types are built with union. Interestingly, a class cannot implement a type with a union, and neither can an interface extend a type with a union. The reason is that it is not possible to know which of the type in the union is actually implemented.

Another difference, which has a bigger impact, is that interface allows to merge multiple definitions together (as described a few pages ago), but not types. This is important because it allows extending outside the library. This technic is used in definition files to open the door to extend missing definitions.

In the end, I recommend using interface for the little advantage of extension on top of type. The only time type has a leverage over interface is when building a type with intersection or union. In that situation, type makes total sense. Also, the documentation still mentions inheritance validity for interface only which may be in motion later and would break inheriting with type. Regardless, any of the two is fine and you should choose the one you are most comfortable with.

9.12 CONSTRUCTOR AKA NEWABLE

An interface can have a construct signature but not an actual constructor. A construct signature is a way to define the shape of the constructor. However, you can define a single construct signature per interface. It starts with the keyword "new", followed by parentheses and parameters to be used by the implemented. A return type can also be specified to mention which interface all members originate from. TypeScript separates static side and instance side of a class. Having an interface that defines the construction is handy since it can be used as a parameter in a constructor function to know which class to instantiate. This construction function can then return the interface that contains the members. The constructor interface can be used in combination with new to instantiate it.

```
interface EntityConstructor {
  new(value: number): EntityInterface;
}
interface EntityInterface {
  functionA(): void;
}

function entityFactory(ctor: EntityConstructor
                      , value: number): EntityInterface {
  return new ctor(value);
}

class EntityA implements EntityInterface {
  constructor(value: number) { }
  functionA(): void {
    console.log("beep beep");
  }
}
class EntityB implements EntityInterface {
  constructor(value: number) { }
  functionA() {
    console.log("tick tock");
  }
}

let digital = entityFactory(EntityA, 1);
let analog = entityFactory(EntityB, 2);
```

9.13 FUNCTION TYPE AKA CALLABLE

A function type resides inside an interface. It describes the shape of the function inside the interface semantic. A synonym is "call signature." The definition is easily distinguishable by having only a signature without a function name. The body of the interface contains one or many functions without a name. The usage of the interface that defines the type of the function remains the same as an interface. However, most of the time, an interface with function type defines the parameter of a function.

```
interface InterfaceNoFuncName {
   (): string; // Function type aka callable
   print(p1: string): void;
}

const MyType = ((): InterfaceNoFuncName => {
   const anyObj: any = (): string => { // Must be ANY!
      return "Returned String";
   }
   anyObj.print = (p1: string) => {
      console.log(p1);
   }
   return anyObj;
}
);
```

With a single function type in the interface, the syntax is simpler to define since a normal function can satisfy the contract. However, when an interface defined multiple function types, closure is required to return an object that will hold the group of functions. The use case for such complex interface may be to pass a specific function as a callback. Such practice with an interface is not a desirable pattern. A class cannot implement interface with an unnamed method signature. It requires using "any" which breaks features like renaming, etc. The only valid use case it to interoperate with existing JavaScript code.

The syntax is like any interface, but inside the interface, you define a function nameless. Callable function supports overload.

```
interface MultipleReturns {
   (s: string): string;
   (i: number): number;
}
```

In practice, this is less used since it's often easier to define an anonymous arrow function signature.

```
    function functionWithFunctionAsParameteAnonymously(p: () => string):
void {
        const s = p();
        console.log(s);
    }
```

9.14 OVERRIDE

TypeScript supports the concept of override. Overriding a function requires a class that extends another class. All base class functions can be overridden if they are not private. To do so, in the subclass you must redefine the method with the exact signature.

```
class OverrideMe {
    public OverrideFunction1(): void {
        console.log("OverrideMe>OverrideFunction1");
    }
    protected OverrideFunction2(): void {
        console.log("OverrideMe>OverrideFunction2");
    }
    private OverrideFunction3(): void {
        console.log("OverrideMe>OverrideFunction3");
    }
}

class Overrider extends OverrideMe {
    public OverrideFunction1(): void {
        console.log("1");
    }
    protected OverrideFunction2(): void {
        console.log("2");
    }
    public callProtected():void{
        this.OverrideFunction2();
    }
}

const overrideClass = new Overrider();
overrideClass.OverrideFunction1(); // Output: 1
overrideClass.callProtected();  // Output: 2
```

One particularity of overriding is that you can still access the base model function. To do so, you must use the keyword “super” followed by the function and the parameters required.

```
public OverrideFunction1(): void {
  console.log("1");
  super.OverrideFunction1();
}
protected OverrideFunction2(): void {
  console.log("2");
  super.OverrideFunction1();
}
```

In the previous example, the output will be four lines. “1” followed by “OverrideMe>OverrideFunction1” and then “2” and “OverrideMe>OverrideFunction2”.

9.15 CONCLUSION

Interfaces are a great way to define a strongly typed group of members. It’s flexible with inheritance way to reuse existing interface without altering existing contracts. The possibility to separate the definition of an interface gives a little edge comparing to type. Finally, a reference to the interface across the system for variables and parameters is a better way than defining anonymous inline types in terms of reusability.

CHAPTER 10: MANIPULATING OBJECT AND ARRAY

10.1 ARRAY WITH SKIP

An array doesn't require to have all their index defined sequentially. It is undefined by default when an index is skipped. There are two ways to have an array that skips element. The first one is when the array is defined. Elements defined between brackets can skip a single element by having two commas next to each other. The second one is to access index on a defined array.

```
const arrskip1 = [0, , , 3, 4];
arrskip1[100] = 100;
arrskip1.forEach((i) => { console.log("{" + i + "}"); });
console.log("This is undefined:" + arrskip1[1]);
```

Output:

```
{0}
{3}
{4}
{100}
This is undefined:undefined
```

10.2 DESTRUCTURING ARRAY

Destructuring an array allows putting data into separated variables, to swap data, or to collect remaining items of an array.

The first case is to move data into a variable. The assignation starts by having on the left side of the equal sign different variables between square brackets, separated by a comma. On the right side, you have the array.

```
let [arr1, arr2] = [1, 2]; // 1 and 2
let [arr3, arr4] = [1, 2, 3, 4]; // 1 and 2
```

You can leverage the rest operator to bring all remaining elements of the array into a smaller array. The accumulation of elements can be useful if you have plenty of data and would like to take a specific set and still hold a reference to the remaining one. A scenario is that you may know that the first three elements contain information at these places all the time but the remaining are dynamically growing or shrinking depending on the scenarios. It's possible to skip some elements by using comma without a variable.

```
let [arr1, arr2] = [1, 2]; // 1 and 2
let [arr3, arr4] = [1, 2, 3, 4]; // 1 and 2
let [arr5, arr6, ...elements] = [1, 2, 3, 4, 5]; // 1 and 2 and [3,4,5]
let [arr7, arr8, , ...elements2] = [1, 2, 3, 4, 5]; // 1 and 2 and [4,5]
```

Furthermore, in destructuring an array, you can swap two variables. You need to have two variables of the same type first. Then, you open the bracket, set the two variables you want to swap separated by a comma, and then close the bracket. Use the equal sign followed by another set of square brackets with the two variables, but this time the order is reversed.

```
let swap1 = 1;
let swap2 = 2;
[swap1, swap2] = [swap2, swap1];
console.log(swap1, swap2); // Output 2 1
```

10.3 DESTRUCTURING OBJECT

Destructuring an object lets you create new variables from an existing object. The syntax starts by using the curly bracket and the name of the destination variable. You can use as many variables separated by commas. The name of the variable must be the name of the members you want to extract from the object that will be selected. Once the selection of member is made, you need to close the curly bracket, use the equal sign and write the name of the variable you want to destruct. In that scenario, like any variable, the use of "let" or "const" was used before starting. Nonetheless, re-deconstruct requires avoiding defining the variable again. However, to use the destructuring, you will have to circumspect the call by parentheses around the whole instruction.

```
const objToDesctruct1 = {
  destr1: 1,
  destr2: "2",
  destr3: true
}
let { destr1, destr2 } = objToDesctruct1;
objToDesctruct1.destr1 *= 100;
({ destr1, destr2 } = objToDesctruct1); // Notice parentheses
```

The second feature goes along with destructuring into variables. You can set specific variables from an object and indicate that all other members not assigned transfers into a new object. The transfer is done using the spread operator on the last variable of the left side of the assignation.

```
const objToDesctruct2 = {
  destr1: 1,
  destr2: "2",
  destr3: true
}
let { destr1, ...remainingObjDestr1} = objToDesctruct1;
/*
let remainingObjDestr1: {
  destr2: string;
  destr3: boolean;
}
*/
```

A third feature is you can name the new variable with something other than the name provided by the member of the original object while destructuring. The same syntax of the first feature renames but with a small twist. The syntax changes by adding a colon after the variable and then the new name. Usually, after the colon, we specify the name, but since you cannot change the name when destructuring, the new name is set.

```
let { destr1: newName } = objToDesctruct1;
console.log(newName);
```

Finally, when destructuring, you may stumble into a member that is optional, in which case, you want to ensure that you have a default value instead. To do so, after the name of the variable, use the equal sign and set the desired default value. TypeScript doesn't use the default value until the value of the parameter is undefined.

```
const objToDesctruct3 = {
  destr1: 1,
  destr2: undefined,
  destr3: true
}
let { destr2: newName2 = "default" } = objToDesctruct3;
console.log("Using default if undefined", newName2); // default
```

10.4 SPREAD OPERATOR & ARRAY

Three dots define the spread operator. It can be used on an array to take every element of the array and to create a copy of each element and return the copy variables. If you spread an array of 10 elements, you will receive a copy of the ten elements positioned one after the other. For example, if you have two arrays and would like to merge them, you could create a new array by opening the square brackets and using the spread operator in front of the first array, followed by a comma and the spread operator followed by the second array before closing the square bracket.

```
const arrOneToBeSpread = [1, 2, 3];
const arrTwoToBeSpread = [4, 5, 6, 7];
const arrCopy = [...arrOneToBeSpread];
const mergedArrCopy = [...arrOneToBeSpread, ...arrTwoToBeSpread];
```

10.5 SPREAD OPERATOR & OBJECT

You can spread an object. Spreading an object is handy in a scenario where you need to create a clone for immutability purposed or if you are already using the function "Object.assign." The "assign" method is similar in functionality but uses a longer form. The syntax for spread operator is identical to the spread for the array which means that it uses the three dots in front of the object instead of the array. Spreading an object will return a shallow copy of all members of the object. To create a clone, you need to define a variable and equal open curly bracket, spread operator, the variable to copy, and close the curly bracket. What it does is it copies all members and have them "floating" side by side with a comma. Indeed, this is just a visualization to help you illustrate that the curly brackets take the result and form a new object.

```
const objToClone = { prop1: 1, prop2: "2" };
const clonedObject = { ...objToClone };
```

Spreading can go a step further. Imagine that you want to add value or multiple values to the cloned new object. It is possible by declaring a new variable, assigning a new object by opening the curly bracket and spreading the object with all the value you have. Instead of closing the curly bracket right away, which would just create a shallow clone, insert a comma and type the name of the property you want to assign to the variable followed by a colon and the value. Close the curly bracket. What happens is that the spread operator will set all members and values, and proceed by setting the members defined after the spread.

```
const objToClone = { prop1: 1, prop2: "2" };
const clonedObject = { ...objToClone };
const clonedObjectWithMore = { ...objToClone, prop3: "3", prop4: false };
```

If the value existed in the spread object and the one manually defined, the latter one would prevail. The cascade is a trick that is often used to have a set of the default values and to let the user override some of the configurations. You could spread a default object followed by a comma and spreading an object with some properties. The result would be a full object with default values where the specified user values have precedence by overriding the default values.

```
const objToClone = { prop1: 1, prop2: "2" };
const clonedObjectWithMore2 = { ...objToClone, prop2: "Override" };
console.log(clonedObjectWithMore2);
// { prop1: 1, prop2: 'Override' }
```

A final last detail to understand is that spreading an object only returns the object's own enumerable properties. The property constraint is important to understand because a rich object (with functions) will lose them. However, if you are manipulating a data object, everything is cloned. A framework like Redux promotes having an immutable store which is formed by many data objects. Cloning with the spread operator is a way to have immutability. The following code demonstrates that having a literal object with a function will be spread but having an object from a class won't be.

```
const objToCloneWithFunction = {
   prop1: 1,
   prop2: "2",
   funct1: function () { console.log("Prop1:", this.prop1); }
};
const clonedObjectWithoutFunc = { ...objToCloneWithFunction };
console.log(clonedObjectWithoutFunc);
//{ prop1: 1, prop2: '2', funct1: [Function: funct1] }

class ClassToClone {
   public funct1() { console.log("Props1:", this.prop1); }
   constructor(public prop1: number, public prop2: string) { }
}
const classToClone = new ClassToClone(1, "2");
const classCloned = { ...classToClone };
console.log(classCloned);
//{ prop1: 1, prop2: '2' }
```

A small modification to the class by adding a function into a variable will make this one available to the cloned object.

```
class ClassToClone2 {
   public funct2 = () => { console.log("Props1:", this.prop1); }
   constructor(public prop1: number, public prop2: string) { }
}
const classToClone2 = new ClassToClone2(1, "2");
const classCloned2 = { ...classToClone2 };
console.log(classCloned2);
// { prop1: 1, prop2: '2', funct2: [Function] }
```

The reason is that the function of the class goes into the prototype, and as mentioned, only members of the object (not the prototype chain) get spread.

10.6 BANG OPERATOR

The bang operator is the use of the exclamation point symbol. The operator can be used after a variable and before the dot to access a member. It is officially called the non-null assertion operator. A variable with the value undefined or null can benefit from using the bang operator because it tells TypeScript that you know that even if the value can theoretically be null or undefined, it's not the case in that particular usage. In a situation where the value cannot be undefined, instead of comparing against null or undefined, you could use the bang operator to access the value. It is important to understand that it can open the door to runtime error and a bang operator is not something you should often see in a project. Under the hood, TypeScript removes from the type of the variable the union with null and undefined.

```
function functionForBang(s: string | undefined): void {
  // console.log("The first letter is ", s.charAt(0)); // Doesn't compile
  console.log("The first letter is ", s!.charAt(0)); // Crash
  const v1 = s;  // v1 type is string | undefined
  const v2 = s!; // v2 type is string
}
functionForBang(undefined);
```

The example above is dangerous because if the parameter is receiving undefined, the code will try to get the first character of an undefined variable. Proper usage is when TypeScript might not infer that in a particular flow of execution, the value cannot be undefined even if the variable is defined to accept undefined. This is true in the case of deferred initialization or re-initialization.

```
let deferedInitialezVariable!: number[];
initialize();
deferedInitialezVariable.push(4);

function initialize(): void {
   deferedInitialezVariable = [0, 1, 2, 3];
}
```

The bang operator must be used carefully.

CHAPTER 11: ASYNCHRONOUS

TypeScript has been supporting the asynchronous syntax since version 1.7 and is available to use even when the output targets version of ECMAScript before version 6. TypeScript syntax is the same as the ECMAScript official version which is to use the keyword "async" before the function which will allow returning a Promise type that is generic. Within the function, you can call other asynchronous functions by using await when the code needs to wait for the end of the execution of the function. It's possible to return a value by using return as well. You can return an async function as well and handle rejected promise by wrapping the await function by a try-and-catch cause. In the end, awaiting a function stops the execution of the async function and waits for the result to come back from the invoked function. It's a simplified way to handle promise.

The example below shows that even if the delays are different, all execution is still done in order. The reason is the keyword "await" that waits for the execution to complete. If you are familiar with Promise, this is similar to have chain all asynchronous function inside "then."

```
function delayMessage(milliseconds: number, message: string)
: Promise<string> {
  return new Promise<string>(resolve => {
    setTimeout(() => { resolve(message); }, milliseconds);
  });
}
async function printWithAsync(): Promise<void> {
  console.log("Start");
  for (let i = 0; i < 10; i++) {
    const randomDelayInMs = Math.floor(50
      + (Math.random() * 5) * 20); // 50-150 ms
    const message = await delayMessage(randomDelayInMs
      , "Msg_" + i + "_" + randomDelayInMs);
    console.log(message);
  }
  console.log("End (after delayed message)");
}
printWithAsync();
/*Start
Msg_0_137
Msg_1_89
Msg_2_141
Msg_3_141
Msg_4_64
Msg_5_56
Msg_6_144
Msg_7_62
Msg_8_79
Msg_9_51
End (after delayed message)*/
```

TypeScript has been supporting Async and Await since version 1.7, with the only constraint being that it's transpilable into ECMAScript 6. However, with version 2.1, TypeScript allows to transpile Async and Await down to ECMAScript 3.

CHAPTER 12: SHARING CODE

Sharing code is the essence of good practice. It allows to build and test once and build on-top of the code in many other projects. TypeScript uses module and namespace to share code as well as definition file.

12.1 NAMESPACE

The concept of namespace in TypeScript is fading away with the second more powerful way to share code that is a module. A namespace is a basic object assigned to the global space. The object, named after the name of the namespace, holds the functions created within this one. TypeScript allows setting code in the namespace across files as well. The goal of using namespace is to structure your code into a logical category and to reduce name collision since the uniqueness is true per namespace only.

The issue around namespace is that as your application grows, the global scope grows as well. It also doesn't offer a way to distribute outside or to break apart an area of your code which you could load dynamically.

A namespace can contain interfaces, classes, types, function, and variable. The keyword "export" opens access outside the boundary of a namespace. Otherwise, the element will be solely available within the namespace. It's important to notice that it is available across files even when not exported as long as within the same namespace.

12.2 MODULE

TypeScript uses the same concept of module specified by ECMAScript 2015. A module is different from namespace in many ways. The first difference is that modules do not use global scope, but their scope. Everything defined within the module is only available in the module to expect if using the keyword "export." A module can load another module by importing using the keyword "import."

A module requires a module loader, of which there are many flavors.

The most common ones are CommonJs, AMD, UMD, System, and ECMAScript.

The separation of the module is per file. A single file is a single module, which means that a code cannot be shared across files. Everything in a file requires using "export" before what it wants to expose. Otherwise, it will be private to the module. A module can contain the same content of a namespace, i.e. interfaces, classes, types, functions, or variables. It's possible to also not specify "export" directly on the element but anywhere in the file by using "export" followed by a curly bracket and the element's name. This might look more verbose, which is true, but it's a way to export something with a different name. That's right; before closing the curly bracket, it's possible to use "as" followed by the desired name to expose.

```
export const module1_variable1 = "test";
export interface module1_interface1 {
  m1: string;
}
```

A module allows exposing other module codes as well. See this feature as a way to proxy the code from multiple modules. This way, you can import a single module and access all other module codes. To create this proxy around a module, you must use "export * from" followed by the module.

```
export * from "./module1";
```

12.2.1 IMPORT MODULE

When it's time to consume a module, you need to import. The import uses the "import" keyword followed by a curly bracket and the name of the exported element. Again, it's possible when importing to rename by using "as" after the exported element name and before closing the curly bracket. Another option is to import everything from the module. Importing a whole module uses the syntax "import * as X from Y" where "Y" is the module and "X" that holds all exports. To access exported an element, you need to use X dot the element.

```
import { module1_variable1, module1_interface1 } from "./module1";
import * as EverythingFromModule1 from "./module1";
console.log(module1_variable1);
console.log(EverythingFromModule1.module1_variable1);
```

12.2.2 DEFAULT EXPORT

Another concept around module is that each module can have a default export. The concept is unique for each module. The syntax is the keyword "default" between "export" and the actual element to expose. A default export opens an import without specifying an element or to load everything with the star syntax. In other words, it allows access by importing without using the curly brackets and exporting without even naming the element. The main use case is exporting a single point of a module.

```
//One file
interface module4Interface { m1: string }
export default module4Interface;

// Another file
import def from "./module4";
const defModule4: def = { m1: "A string" };
```

The export doesn't need to export a function or a variable that has a name. It doesn't matter because it is the import that defines under which identifier the default element is referenced.

```
export default (input: number) => input * 10;
```

12.2.3 LAZY LOADING MODULE < 2.4

TypeScript analyzes the code while transpiling into JavaScript and can detect when an import is being used only for its type or not. Removing code is an important notion which helps to remove the size of the bundle of dependencies. It is also important if you want to lazy load a module.

Lazy loading is the principle of loading on-demand when the module is required. Lazy loading gives a performance boost by only initially loading what is needed. Hereafter, the lazy loading pattern can load additional module for a particular route or for particular actions. Lazy loading support is still in an infantile stage with a syntax that requires being closer to a specific module target. For example, a way to do it with TypeScript is to import using "require." Inside the function that uses the lazily loaded module, the code calls "require" to create an element of the module and mark its type with "typeof" with the imported type at the top of the file. This line of code must set the value by calling require again.

```
import module1_variable1 = require("./module1");
export function lazyLoadWhenInvoked() {
   const _foo: typeof module1_variable1 = require("./module1");
   console.log(_foo.module1_variable1);
}
lazyLoadWhenInvoked();
```

12.2.4 LAZY LOADING MODULE >=2.4

Lazy loading can also use a dynamic import expression which is a recent feature of ECMAScript. However, this time, a promise syntax is supported which allows having the module in the "then" or the exception detail in the "catch". To do so, TypeScript's configurations must specify "esnext" as module and target "es5" or higher. Some modules still do not completely support the syntax and require to have TypeScript configured to use the "moduleResolution" to "node."

```
async function getVariableLazyLoaded1(): Promise<string> {
   const mod1 = await import("./module1");
   const varFromOtherModule = await mod1.module1_variable1;
   return Promise.resolve(varFromOtherModule);
}
```

Or without async and only using a promise.

```
function getVariableLazyLoaded2(): Promise<string> {
  return import("./module1").then(mod1 => {
    return mod1.module1_variable1;
  });
}
```

It's also possible to combine lazily loaded package with Webpack. The use of "import" can use the comment approach to specify in which bundle to pack the desired module that is specified in the import statement.

```
return import(/* webpackChunkName: "bundleAbc" */"./module1").then(...
```

12.2.5 IMPORT SHORTCUT

TypeScript's configuration can create shortcuts to specific areas of the code. A shortcut can be useful in a situation where many imports are deep in another branch of the code which requires much navigation down; for example "/../../../../...". To set up a shortcut, the TypeScript's configuration needs to have a "baseUrl" in the "tsconfig.json." Then, it's possible to add many shortcuts. Each of the shortcuts goes in the "paths" list and is relative to the "baseUrl." The definition of each path contained is a keys-values list, for which the key is the pattern to look for when importing and the value is the location to look for at the actual TypeScript file. The configuration can look like the following:

```
"baseUrl": "./src",
"paths": {
  "@link/folder1/*": ["folderInSrc/a/b/c/folder1/*"],
  "@link/folder2/*": ["folderInSrc/x/y/z/*"]
}

import { class1 } from "@link/folder1/file123"
```

The paths' keys don't need to start with an @, but it's a good way to differentiate between shortcuts and actual paths.

12.3 DEFINITION FILE

TypeScript works seamlessly with JavaScript code because of the definition file concept. Definition files contain the type of each public function or variable that an external module not written in Typescript offers. The most popular definition file is probably lib.d.ts which contains thousands of lines of definition about the core functionalities of JavaScript. It comes with TypeScript, and you shouldn't have to care much else that it provides Intellisense because it contains types of ECMAScript core language functions and variables; for example, the definition of the function "parseFloat."

TypeScript's configuration allows adding other "system" libraries. It works as a supplement to the core feature of a specific ECMAScript target; for example, the "promise" library which allows developing with a library not yet incorporated inside any core ECMAScript target. Adding a system library requires changing the tsconfig.json under "lib." Projects automatically add libraries from the lib's files. Unlike modules, lib doesn't need the keyword "import." You can dive into the lib.d.ts file by going to the definition (F12 in most IDEs). It opens the definition file at the variables, functions, or types that has focus. Exploring libraries under "lib" is a great way to learn what ECMAScript and ECMAScript's neighbor libraries contain. The lib.d.ts changes depending on the selected target defined in TypeScript configuration.

12.3.1 GLOBAL DEFINITION FILE

Another common definition file is globals.d.ts. It's an extension to lib.d.ts. Any addition to this file is globally available. However, it is better to have a custom definition file per module not to mix different non-related definitions. The globals.d.ts is an option for cases where you need to change something from the JavaScript library. Since JavaScript lets you modify, add, or remove a declaration to the core library, TypeScript must also support a way to type any change to the core library. The use of global.d.ts brings all the modifications in a single file. However, globals.d.ts is not the only place that can affect the global score. In fact, the use of "declare global" and the interface within the curly bracket set the definition in the global scope.

12.3.2 DECLARE AND DEFINITION FILE

In the section about declaration, we briefly introduced the use of the keyword "declare." Definition files often use "declare" to mention that a variable exists, not declared in this file per se, but exists as a specific type. That's is right; since many variables, e.g. "window" or "Math", do exist beyond Typescript, in JavaScript. Most of the types in lib.d.ts use interface as well. The justification to use interface is because of its property of being extensional. The extension feature goes along with globals.d.ts, which allows modifying a core interface already defined. It leverages the interface feature that merges multiple definitions with lib.d.ts.

12.3.3 REPOSITORY OF DEFINITION FILES

You can get definition files from two different places. The first one, getting more popular, is directly from the JavaScript library when installing through NPM. If you look at the downloaded package, you might see index.d.ts in the folder of the library. If that is the case, it means that the author of the JavaScript library is providing the definition file. Having the library include the definition is the best case because the definition file is always in sync and up-to-date with the code. The second way to get a definition file is to use NPM with @types/X where X is the name of the library you want the definition file from. The NPM package is not automatically valid for every library, but thousands and thousands of libraries got a package just for the type. The source code is from GitHub under the repository "DefinitelyTyped," and it contains a collection of definition files across all libraries that contributors give their time to, to keep the definition files up-to-date. Definition files are installed under the node_modules folder, under the folder "@types," inside the folder of the library requested. The TypeScript transpiler knows to look up in this folder. The location can also change in the compiler configuration file.

12.3.4 GENERATING A DEFINITION FILE

An author of a library in JavaScript that wants types, for TypeScript consumers, need to write a definition file. There is no magic to autogenerate the definition file, and it can involve quite a considerable amount of time to set up a file, depending on how big the library is. If you wrote your code in TypeScript, it's possible to produce the definition file directly when compiling but using the "declaration" option to true. By doing so, you'll end up having a single definition file for your project all typed for you. Using the compiler is the quickest way. Since TypeScript knows the type of your project during compilation, all that information can be used to produce the definition file. The produced definition file can be copied and packaged with the JavaScript in the published package.

12.3.5 JAVASCRIPT WITHOUT DEFINITION FILE

In case there is no definition file available and you have no desire to create one, you need to create a fake definition file.

```
Could not find a declaration file for module
```

This fake definition file lets you use the imported JavaScript file but won't give you any types. TypeScript needs to know about this file. The configuration file needs to have an entry to the location of the folder where the fake definition file resides.

The following example gets the library "pad" with NPM. Let's pretend that there is no definition file. The first step is to create in the @types folder a folder with the name of the library "pad", and then a file named "index.d.ts" with the following code.

```
declare module "pad";
```

The code can import the library and execute the code. No Intellisense or type protection is provided since the definition file is defining nothing else that "pad" is a module.

```
import * as pad from "pad";
console.log(pad("Test", 25, '+'));
```

Finally, TypeScript must know the location of the definition files. The configuration file lets you include the path for definition file like any other TypeScript files. Moreover, TypeScript will check for the @types folder.

```
"include": [
  "src/**/*.ts",
  "@types/**/*.d.ts"
]
```

12.4 CODE AND TEST

TypeScript configuration lets you specify which module target you want to use. That means that you can use it for your web development AMD and your test CommonJs without having to change your code. The transpiler takes care to render the correct syntax for the targeted module system.

CHAPTER 13: DECORATORS

A decorator is a reusable piece of code that allows injection of logic by writing a single line. The concept exists in JavaScript, and TypeScript allows implementation of Decorator regardless of which ECMAScript version is making the adoption of decorator not browser-specific. Again, TypeScript shines by opening the door to advanced features by generating polyfill. A decorator is easily recognizable because it uses a commercial at the sign: @.

It's important to understand that a decorator acts differently depending on their association which forges different types. We will see in more details every type of decorator. Know that, for the moment, we can create a decorator that can hook on classes, methods, properties, accessor, and parameters.

TypeScript needs two configurations to be true to access every type of accessors. The first step is to change the "tsconfig.json" file to add two properties.

```
"experimentalDecorators": true,
"emitDecoratorMetadata": true,
```

The experimentDecorator allows to use decorator in TypeScript, and the emitDecorator generates the proper JavaScript decorator.

13.1 CLASS DECORATOR

A class decorator is applied to the class definition. The decorator's constructor uses a single parameter which is the decorated class. The constructor function attaches to the prototype and hence requires some additional codes if the goal is to do action on each instance creation. To manipulate the creation of instance, the decorator class must return a wrapped version of the constructor. Here is an example of a strongly typed function that wraps the construction of any class with the decorator.

```
export function countinstance<T
  extends { new(...args: any[]): {} }>
  (constructor: T) {
  console.log("This is called once per class type");
  const wrapper = class extends constructor {
    public static instanceCount = 0;

    constructor(...args: any[]) {
      super();
      wrapper.instanceCount++;
      console.log("Called every instantiation. Count = " +
                  wrapper.instanceCount);
    }
  }
  return wrapper;
}
```

To use a decorator on a class, a function must take a constructor of type 'T' that extends any arguments. This way, it will be able to bind to any class construction. The idea is that the decorator's function will shim between the actual class and the decorator. The static count on the object that the function returns is a class which has the property that increases with each instantiation, with each time wrapper calls.

To use this class decorator, you need to use @countinstance on top of the class. The decorator uses a static variable to count the instance, and every time the class is instantiated, the count increases.

```
@countinstance
class OneClassWithDecorator{

}
const classDeco1 = new OneClassWithDecorator();
const classDeco2 = new OneClassWithDecorator();
```

In the example above, the notion of decorator associated with the prototype appears. The first call to the output methods executes once. The execution appears when JavaScript discovers the class. You can comment out the two instantiations, and the console will print. However, the second console print calls only at the creation of the object. Again, this is because the wrapper got attached when JavaScript found the class and the decorator and now a proxy calls the console and the incrementation of the variable on every instantiation.

13.2 METHOD DECORATOR

```
export function autobind(
  target: Object
  , key: string | symbol
  , descriptor: PropertyDescriptor)
  : PropertyDescriptor {
  const fn = descriptor.value;
  return {
    configurable: true,
    get() {
      const boundFn = fn.bind(this);
      Object.defineProperty(this, key, {
        value: boundFn,
        configurable: true,
        writable: true
      });
      return boundFn;
    }
  };
}
```

As you can see, the function's signature is different from the class one. The signature takes a target, a key, and a descriptor argument. The target is the instance, the key is the method, and the descriptor contains a reference to the function.

Again, as you can see, the first line takes the function and inside the return "get" function we use the "bind" on the function with the "this" reference. That's it. To create a class that hooks on NodeJs event for which we do not use the decorator, the "this" will be the context and refer to an undefined value. The decorator @autobind changes the pointer "this" to reference the class anytime a function uses the decorator.

```
class ClassDecoratorWithMethod {
   private x: string = "ValueHere";
   constructor() {
      process.on("uncaughtException", this.eventCallback);
      throw Error("My error"); // Will call the callback from previous line
   }
   @autobind
   private eventCallback(): void {
      console.log("This is not window but the class", this.x);
   }
}

const classDecoWithMeth = new ClassDecoratorWithMethod();
// Without Decorator:
// This is not window but the class ValueHere
// With Decorator:
// This is not window but the class undefined
```

13.3 ACCESSOR DECORATOR

The accessor decorator marks the setters or getters of a class. It allows to read the value from the property descriptor and to modify this one.

```
function capitalize() {
   return (
      target: Object
      , key: string | symbol
      , descriptor: PropertyDescriptor
   ) => {
      const originalGet = descriptor.get;
      if (originalGet !== undefined) {
         descriptor.get = function () {
            return (() => {
               const valueFromOriginal =
                  originalGet.call(this) as string;
               return valueFromOriginal.toUpperCase();
            })();
         };
      }
   };
}
```

The decorator wraps in a function a return statement that takes a target, a property key, and a property descriptor. The original accessor is accessible, and the idea is to define an enhanced version of the getter or setter without the need for modification to the original one. During invocation of an accessor with a decorator, the decorator acts as a proxy. The execution path is the decorator and then the original if the decorator calls the original. That's right; a decorator can skip the original.

```
class ClassWithAccessorDecorator {
  public constructor(private myString: string) {
  }

  @capitalize()
  public get format(): string {
    return this.myString;
  }
}
const objAccessorDecorator = new ClassWithAccessorDecorator("test");
console.log("String value", objAccessorDecorator.format);
// String value TEST
```

In the example above, the decorator assumes that the function uses the decorator on a string accessor and upper case the original string. The result is possible because the decorator sets a new ".get" function, hence shims the actual getter. It still calls the original getter to get the actual value, but alters the value before returning the capitalized value.

13.4 PROPERTY DECORATOR

The second decorator acts on a property by using the reflect package. Using reflect package requires adding impost "reflect-metadata" at the top of the decorator file, hence the need to use "NPM install --save-dev reflect-metadata". This library gives us some capability in terms of reading information reflexively. A decorator on a property requires two functions, instead of one, like for class or accessor decorator: One function that reads the decorator assigned to the property and one that reads the value and assigns the value. It's important to understand that the decorator won't be useful when the property is accessed (neither when setting or getting a value directly). The decorator can be used on a property and can only be leveraged by a function. You can see this kind of decorator as a way to provide metadata to properties and opening the door to have something else to consume this metadata in conjunction with the value of the property.

```
import "reflect-metadata";
const formatMetadataKey = Symbol("format");

// Decorator to use on property
export function stringCoater(formatString: string, star: number) {
   const stringToUse = Array(star).join("*")
   + formatString
   + Array(star).join("*");
   return Reflect.metadata(formatMetadataKey, stringToUse);
}

// Read the decorator from the property
export function getFormat<T>(
   target: Object
   , propertyKey: keyof T
): string {
   return Reflect.getMetadata(formatMetadataKey, target, propertyKey);
}
```

The example provides a way to specify a format that will coat a string property with stars. A property can assign the decorator "stringCoater." The "getFormat" function allows for reading the decorator.

```
class DecoratorOnProperty {
   @stringCoater("[%s]", 10)
   public title: string;
   constructor(title: string) { this.title = title; }
   public getFormattedTitle(): string {
      const formatString = getFormat<DecoratorOnProperty>(this, "title");
      return formatString.replace("%s", this.title);
   }
}
const objDecoProp = new DecoratorOnProperty("Test");
console.log("Out", objDecoProp.getFormattedTitle());
// Out *********[Test]*********
```

The example uses the decorator in a formatted function. The first line reads the property and the second takes the value of the property and assigns it to the placeholder %S.

13.5 PARAMETER DECORATOR

The parameter decorator requires multiple functions. But before diving into the required function, we need to define the symbol. During code reflection, the symbol enters into play to see if a parameter has the decorator to apply the validation or not. The following example creates a decorator that will throw an exception if the value of the decorated parameter is null. Let's call the decorator "notnull" but it could be any name. The variable created from the symbol links the two functions.

The first decorator function specifies which parameter the second function must act on. The second function is the decorator that sits on top of the function where the first decorator marks a parameter. That's right; we need to have one decorator for the function and one for the parameter. The reason is that we want to gather all parameters with the symbol we defined (for notnull) and to apply the validation when the method is invoked.

The second function is to do the heavy lifting. First, it looks to get all parameters' index that needs to check for null or undefined. The role of the first function is to mark the parameter for null or undefined. All parameters with the decorator are kept in memory by their index. The second piece of this function is to loop through the selected argument from the list built and check if the value is null. If the value is null: throw an exception.

```
import "reflect-metadata";
const notnullMetadataKey = Symbol("notnull");

export function notnull(
  target: Object
  , propertyKey: string | symbol
  , parameterIndex: number) {
  let existingRequiredParameters: number[]
    = Reflect.getOwnMetadata(notnullMetadataKey, target, propertyKey)
    || [];
  existingRequiredParameters.push(parameterIndex);
  Reflect.defineMetadata(notnullMetadataKey
    , existingRequiredParameters, target, propertyKey);
}

export function validatenotnull(target: Object
  , propertyName: string
  , descriptor: TypedPropertyDescriptor<Function>) {
  const originalMethod = descriptor.value;
  if (originalMethod !== undefined) {
    descriptor.value = function (...args: any[]) {
      const requiredParameters: number[]
        = Reflect.getOwnMetadata(notnullMetadataKey
          , target, propertyName);
      if (requiredParameters) {
        for (const parameterIndex of requiredParameters) {
          const valueOfParameter = args[parameterIndex];
          if (valueOfParameter === undefined
            || valueOfParameter === null) {
            const types = Reflect.getMetadata("design:paramtypes"
              , target, propertyName) as object[];
            throw new Error("Missing required argument name at index '"
              + parameterIndex + "' of type '"
              + types[parameterIndex].toString()
              + "'. Value is '" + valueOfParameter + "'.");
          }
        }
      }
      return originalMethod.apply(this, args);
    }
  }
  return undefined;
}
```

Here is an example of using the decorator and having that one thrown the Error exception.

```
class DecoratorOnParameter {
  @validatenotnull
  public concatenate(@notnull s1?: string, s2: string = ""): string {
    return s1 + s2;
  }
}
const objDecoParam = new DecoratorOnParameter();
objDecoParam.concatenate(undefined);
```

CHAPTER 14: MIXIN

A mixin is a technic used in JavaScript to extend features to existing class (ECMAScript/TypeScript class or JavaScript function that behaves as a class) without using inheritance but instead composition. Mixin brings flexibility by enhancing dynamically, instead of statically, the definition of a class. Mixin comes with the drawback of having the order of execution being harder to read and harder to anticipate but brings an interesting pattern for dynamic members aggregation. A mixin is especially powerful if you have a class that inherits a different base class depending on the context. The pattern is different from traditional object-oriented where a class can inherit only a single and static type.

14.1 CLASS MIXIN

A mixin is a function that takes a parameter as a class with a constructor and returns a new class. We are talking about class and not object. That means the result of a mixin requires being instantiated before invoked. It also means that the result of a mixin function can be used on another mixin. This allows chaining the mixin to merge several implementations to the initial class. Multiple chains of mixing can be viewed as multiple inheritances.

To create a mixin, you need to first set up a generic type where the generic is a class. TypeScript has the keyword "type" and creates an unnamed generic function that takes a list of any parameter. The function needs to have "new" in its definition to make it a constructor function which is what lets a class pass. Every class must have a constructor even if not explicitly defined. The mixin function is a generic one, and the generic type extends the constructor type. The code of the mixin is a return followed by "class" which extends the parameter variable which in itself is a generic type of mixin.

```
type Constructor<T = {}> = new (...args: any[]) => T;

// Mixing without a constructor
// Add a "do" function
function Runner<TBase extends Constructor>(Base: TBase) {
  return class Timestamped extends Base {
    private speed = 10;
    public do = () => {
      console.log("Run at the pace of " + this.speed)
    };
  };
}
```

Mixins can also have their constructor. They can also define a function without being variable like standard class. One caveat is that the constructor must have an array of any argument.

```
// Mixin with a constructor
// Add a "do" function (or override if Runner is used)
// Add a "stop" function
function Walker<TBase extends Constructor>(Base: TBase) {
  return class Timestamped extends Base {
    private speed: number;
    constructor(...args: any[]) {
      super(...args);
      this.speed = 5;
    }
    public do = () => {
      console.log("Walk at the pace of " + this.speed)
    };

    public stop(): void {
      console.log("Walk has stopped");
      this.speed = 0;
    }
  };
}
```

When using a chain of mixin, if the latter defines the same members, it will override the former. Here is an example that creates a class and will apply two mixins in a different order. The result is different since they both have the same "do" function. Notice how the class is not aware of the mixin and the separation allows any class to host the mixin.

```
class Player {
  name: string;

  constructor(name: string) {
    this.name = name;
  }
}

const PlayerThatCanRunWalk = Walker(Runner(Player));
const PlayerThatCanWalkRun = Runner(Walker(Player));
const user1 = new PlayerThatCanRunWalk("Patrick");
const user2 = new PlayerThatCanWalkRun("Patrick");
user1.do();
user1.stop();
user2.do();
user2.stop();
// Walk at the pace of 5
// Walk has stopped
// Run at the pace of 10
// Walk has stopped
```

14.2 FUNCTION MIXIN

We have seen that it's possible to define mixin using a function that returns a class wrapped around an existing class. However, it's also possible to avoid returning a class and to inject the prototype chain with new functions.

The first step is to extract the function to use in the mixin into an interface. This will allow separating the implementation from the contract that we want to expose. In this way of using a mixin, the original class must implement the interface but will wait the mixin to take over the implementation. That means that it's less flexible than the first approach, which can be a positive aspect if you want to control what is allowed to use specific mixins. The second step is to implement the interfaces to have concrete mixins.

```
// Disposable Mixin
interface IDisposable {
  dispose(): void;
}
class Disposable implements IDisposable {
  isDisposed: boolean;
  dispose() {
    this.isDisposed = true;
  }

}

// Activatable Mixin
interface IActivatable {
  isActive: boolean;
  activate: () => void;
  deactivate: () => void;

}
class Activatable implements IActivatable {
  isActive: boolean;
  activate() {
    this.isActive = true;
  }
  deactivate() {
    this.isActive = false;
  }
}
```

The third step is to create a utility function that takes the original class that implements the interfaces and a collection of mixins to apply. This function is generic and can be used across all your projects. What it does is a simple loop on the mixin and for each mixin transferring their properties into the original class. Finally, the fourth step is to apply the mixin and instantiate the class.

```
// Mixin utility functions
function applyMixins(derivedCtor: any, baseCtors: any[]) {
  baseCtors.forEach(baseCtor => {
    Object.getOwnPropertyNames(baseCtor.prototype).forEach(name => {
      derivedCtor.prototype[name] = baseCtor.prototype[name];
    });
  });
}

// Apply mixin
class ClassThatUseBothMixin implements IDisposable, IActivatable {
  // Disposable
  isDisposed: boolean = false;
  dispose: () => void;
  // Activatable
  isActive: boolean = false;
  activate: () => void;
  deactivate: () => void;
}
applyMixins(ClassThatUseBothMixin, [Disposable, Activatable]);

// Usage
let smartObj = new ClassThatUseBothMixin();
```

It's important to understand that applying a mixin or mixins to class will do it permanently since it changes the prototype chain.

CHAPTER 16: JAVASCRIPT

TypeScript has the capability of analyzing JavaScript files if desired. Reading JavaScript works by using TypeScript's inference as well as understanding definition file from libraries when available. Using TypeScript with JavaScript files is a common practice when transferring from JavaScript with the goal of having at some point a code base coded in TypeScript. It's a temporary state in which TypeScript shines by having a hybrid of JavaScript and TypeScript.

By default, TypeScript only reads files ending with a .ts extension. However, by changing the compiler option "allowJs" to true, every JavaScript file will be analyzed. That means that at the end, TypeScript will output something similar to the JavaScript written but it doesn't mean that it will be the same. For example, if you are using "const" and you target ECMAScript version 3, the compilation will change all constants ("const") to "var." The purpose is dual. It can transform the JavaScript, and it can also be a static analyzer. To be able to have the second part, the option "checkJs" must also be true. The combination of the two is powerful, transforming JavaScript into the direction of being as strict as TypeScript can be.

Setting both compiler options "allowJs" and "checkJs" to "true" may be too radical. Without any other indication to TypeScript's compiler, every JavaScript file becomes analyzed. To reduce the scope, it's possible to use two strategies. The first strategy is to set "allowJs" to true, and "checkJs" to true. Next, use the comment "// @ts-nocheck" at the top of files that you do not want TypeScript to analyze. The combination of the three configurations lets TypeScript transform the JavaScript without validation for cherry-picked files. In the same mindset, it's possible to ignore a specific line instead of a full file by using "// @ts-ignore". A second strategy is to "allowJs" to true and "checkJs" to false. TypeScript will read the files but not analyze the file. However, adding at the top of the file the comment "//@ts-check" gives TypeScript the hint to analyze the marked file. Partial analyzing is good when a progressive transformation is required and when too many files require modification before swapping definitely to

Typescript.

To reiterate, "allowJs" allows TypeScript to read JavaScript file to be transformed by TypeScript. CheckJs allows for static analysis by inference and with definition files.

INDEX

K

L

M

N

O

P

R

S

T

U

V

ABOUT THE AUTHOR

Patrick Desjardins has been working for Netflix as a senior software developer engineer since 2017 and is also a former senior software developer engineer at Microsoft, working on MSDN, VSTS, and Teams. He was a Microsoft Most Valuable Professional (MVP) in Asp.Net for two consecutive years, 2013 and 2014. He studied software engineering and is known for his analysis, resourcefulness, and ability to find effective solutions quickly. Since his early professional career, his focus has always been to keep up to date in order to provide quality services to meet customers' needs. Patrick is a professional who has a well-developed work ethic and who has the desire to perform both in quality and timeliness. His area of interest is Web development, which he has embraced since the early 2000s. For many years, Patrick has continued to train daily in new technologies and seeks to apply all theories learned to various projects. Patrick is a huge fan of Microsoft technologies' .Net which he used to develop professionally since 2004. By contrast, in 2002 he started to develop many projects in PHP, which makes him someone with multiple perspectives on how the web can be developed. His main focus is to help people to embrace Microsoft technology in an enterprise environment. He is a strong believer of the .NET ecosystem, TypeScript, and React to help create quality web and follow good standards with Html5, CSS3, unit testing, and design patterns.

BACK PAGE

WHAT YOU WILL LEARN

This book is for people with an interest to improve their development velocity by using static typing with Typescript. A basic understanding of JavaScript and web development is suggested. This book doesn't cover how to develop client-side code but explores TypeScript features. TypeScript concepts are explained and every chapter is a dig deeper into useful features that will simplify, clarify and disentangle your code. The goal is to delve into the core potential of TypeScript to help you leverage all the benefits of static typing code in a web environment. Topics covered but not limited to are:

- Features up to TypeScript 2.8 version
- Transpiler's configurations
- Basis JavaScript in TypeScript
- Object and Object-Oriented
- Functions, Modules, and Asynchronous Code
- Interfaces, Types and more!

ABOUT THE AUTHOR

Patrick Desjardins is a senior software engineer at Netflix and a former senior software engineer at Microsoft who worked on MSDN, Visual Studio Online, and Microsoft Teams. Patrick is an author of many books, a creator of several online classes, an inventor with several patents, and an international speaker on web technologies.

www.ingramcontent.com/pod-product-compliance
Lightning Source LLC
LaVergne TN
LVHW042335060326
832902LV00006B/177

* 9 7 8 2 9 8 1 3 1 1 0 6 1 *